Vanessa Berry | Ninety 9

Vanessa Berry

GIRAMONDO

Ninety 9

First published 2013
from the Writing & Society Research Group
at the University of Western Sydney
by the Giramondo Publishing Company
PO Box 752
Artarmon NSW 1570 Australia
www.giramondopublishing.com

Text and Illustrations © Vanessa Berry 2013

Designed by Harry Williamson
Typeset by Andrew Davies
in 10/14.5 pt Minion Pro
Printed and bound by Ligare Book Printers
Distributed in Australia by NewSouth Books

National Library of Australia
Cataloguing-in-Publication data:

Berry, Vanessa
Ninety 9
ISBN 9781922146328 (pbk)

391.475

Contents

Teen Spirit

In 1990 I was 11 years old and the last decade of the millennium stretched before me. Whatever happened in these years would shape the adult I was to become.

At the start of 1990 my mother, sister and I moved to a house in Turramurra. The three of us had, for a few years, been living with my grandparents, after my parents separated in the late 1980s. Now this interim phase was over and we were living in a house of our own again. Turramurra was a quiet, well-to-do Sydney suburb known for nothing more exciting than having the greatest average rainfall of any region in the city. Our small brick house on a rectangle of lawn was the kind of unremarkable place I would never have noticed before it became our home.

I started high school with the knowledge that I would forever be too weird to be popular. My childhood had been spent obsessing over things like flamenco dancers and Russian fairy tales such as Vassillisa the Beautiful; the story of a girl with a magic doll which helps her to outsmart Baba Yaga, the forest witch. At school I did my best to fit in, expressing love for Kylie Minogue songs when asked, and even making up a love interest when it seemed like the right thing to do. But my fake boyfriend – with his skateboard, ripped jeans and messy blonde hair – could do little to hide my true self.

High school and the 1990s seemed destined to continue the theme that had dominated my life up until that point: I operated on a different

wavelength to other people my age. I sometimes wondered if I had been meant to live in the 1880s but had arrived in 1980s instead. I had read about this kind of time switch in books like *Playing Beattie Bow* or *Charlotte Sometimes*: it often happened to girls who were outsiders. Despite my attempts to fit in, at school I mostly hid behind a deep shyness. This too aroused people's attention: my weird quietness was pointed out to me by plenty of primary school bullies and the odd sadistic PE teacher. At school I had more in common with the axolotl that lived in the tank in the corner of the classroom than any of my peers. I'd stare at it languishing at the bottom of its tank and think: I know how you feel.

One Saturday afternoon in late 1991 my younger sister, Fiona, was making a cake. My bedroom was next to the kitchen and the telephone table, where the olive-green phone with rotary dial and curly cord sat amid a pile of scrawled notes, junk mail, and general debris. Our house, unlike the houses of my school friends, was forever cluttered. Amid the jumble of objects on the yellow kitchen bench, Fiona was sifting flour into the bright red melamine mixing bowl that had produced every cake baked in our family for as long as I could remember.

By this point in my life I'd found something that made me feel tethered to the here and now, rather than floating in a timeless personal fairytale of Spanish dresses and Baba Yaga. In 1991 I, like many teenage girls across Australia, had seen the video for 'That Ain't Bad' by Ratcat on Saturday morning *Video Hits* and become smitten. The video was all black except for the faces of the band and the oversized heart of Simon Day's red Rickenbacker, and the song was a seesaw of buzzing guitar and the repeated 'I love you's of the chorus. The magic of this pale, handsome boy, tossing his long black hair around, mouthing 'I love you' to me, was interspersed with a few black and white scenes of the band walking around Pyrmont.

Watching the three guys in their leather jackets walking underneath the monorail track and the construction sites on the city's edge was as an important, if less titillating, detail as Simon Day's good looks. These cool, handsome boys, with their black jeans, boots and guitars, lived in the same city as me. Australia was so remote from the places I saw on television or heard celebrated in pop songs. London, Los Angeles, New York: they were unreal, glamorous spectres that felt inaccessible except in daydreams. When I flipped through the art textbook that had been purchased for my coming year of school I took note of the Surrealist Map of the World, in which Australia was a tiny, shrunken shape at the bottom.

It was exciting to think that there were more adventurous and mysterious sides to Sydney. Like most children from the suburbs I'd taken a ride on the monorail after it opened in 1988. It was still new enough to seem part of the future city Sydney would one day become. In the Ratcat video it had a new identity as the backdrop to urban adventures. It was a glimpse of the world that lay on the other side of the Harbour Bridge, in which I imagined people wore black, played in bands, and roamed around the city at night. I imagined a different, older, better dressed, and far cooler version of myself out exploring with them.

The majority of the music which dominated the charts in the late 1980s and early 1990s was either corny soft rock designed for love song dedications – 'More than Words' by Extreme or 'Everything I Do (I do it for you)' by Bryan Adams – or songs manufactured to appeal to young people, like the unconvincing 'Ice Ice Baby' by Vanilla Ice. I could only imagine boy bands like New Kids on the Block, who were marketed as a teenage girls' dream, teasing people like me from the back of the bus. A band like Ratcat seemed far more real.

Ratcat's crossover success in 1991 was a premonition of a greater shift that would soon occur in pop music, a shift marked by one iconic song. I first heard it as Fiona made the cake in the kitchen that afternoon. I was listening to Triple J on the double cassette/radio player that had initially been bought to assist Fiona's opera singing practice. I had moved it to my room and repurposed it into my cultural lifeline. From the speakers a song called out to me. 'Hello,' it said, 'hello, hello hello, how low?'

Three and a half years later I would answer the olive-green rotary dial phone and hear from my friend Penny that Kurt Cobain was dead, but for now Kurt Cobain was greeting me and the world, only to tell us: oh well, whatever, nevermind. I turned the radio up and made my sister listen.

As compelling as the song was, I wanted to know what it was that we were never to mind about. By the time I first heard 'Smells Like Teen Spirit' I had been avidly listening to music all year. The fuzzy guitars of Ratcat led me to other Sydney bands like The Hummingbirds and The Clouds, to English bands like The Jesus and Mary Chain and My Bloody Valentine. I was beginning to explore a vast musical family tree and the further I went, the more I discovered. Alternative music seemed a place where misfits like me might belong; I felt connected with the present time in a way I never had before.

One night I was listening to Simon Day program his five favourite songs on Triple J and he selected 'To Here Knows When' by My Bloody Valentine. Airy, sweet-nothing vocals glided above a thicket of guitars, a sound equally as heavy as it was soft. Even the name My Bloody Valentine was like a magic spell going to work on me. From here I discovered other British bands like Ride, Lush and Swervedriver,

and the word coined to describe them: shoegaze. The name had come about due to their introspective stage presence, looking down at their guitars and effects pedals as they played. These songs of floating, layered guitars were the opposite to the clean sounds of early 90s chart pop, and it was this direction I wanted to go.

Although I was only partially aware of it at the time, I was part of a cultural shift which occurred in the early 1990s, in which previously underground sounds and scenes were displaced from their inner-city enclaves and dispersed to suburban teenagers. Some who were part of these scenes felt as if their cultures had been overrun or even destroyed and wrote angry letters to the street press about teenyboppers and fashion victims. Although I was new to it, I never felt as if I was just jumping on a fashionable bandwagon. I was grateful for this music. It was a place for misfits and outsiders, where being different was desirable. I felt as if I was peeling back a layer from my surroundings to reveal another kind of life. This music was a pathway to a whole other way of being, a secret world to explore.

Band T-shirt

In the 1990s, band T-shirts were a kind of code, allowing you to reveal your secret identity to others. Your secret identity was a person of discerning taste, who spurned the 'mainstream' and had a deep understanding of the perils of being like everyone else. Sightings of someone wearing a Superchunk or Butthole Surfers T-shirt could inspire a thrill, almost a panic, that you were not alone.

Before I wore band T-shirts, my style was a mismatch of influences, inspired by such diverse sources as my high school art teacher who wore fluoro tutus and spiked her black hair up like a pineapple, and Ally Sheedy as the 'basket case' girl in *The Breakfast Club* with her shapeless

black clothes and hair covering her eyes. Then, when I became a music fan, my choices were inevitable. Every band I heard on the radio seemed to have a T-shirt to match.

The first band shirt I owned was a Cure shirt. As many teenagers do, I felt despair over my appearance which was awkwardly young no matter what I wore. I never seemed to be able to choose clothes that fitted in with other people my age and I soon stopped trying. My first act of rebellion was painting my denim shorts with Ratcat-inspired hearts and daggers, rolling them up and wearing them with hot pink tights. Realising this outfit would not be approved of at home, before going out I packed it in my bag and changed into it in the train station toilets, like Stephanie Kaye from *Degrassi Junior High* who would switch her long skirts for hotpants once she arrived at school.

Music had fast become the most important thing in my life and The Cure was my first deep musical obsession. Unlike Ratcat's limited back catalogue, The Cure had a whole world of albums and phases to explore. I'd first discovered them through the 1990 video for 'Close to Me', a reprise of the 1986 original. In the original video the band is confined inside a wardrobe on the edge of a cliff, which then plummets to the rocks below. The 1990 video, which accompanied a remix of the song, continued the story. The band slowly float out from the wardrobe and explore the undersea world as an octopus plays multiple saxophones and tries to strangle Robert Smith with one of its tentacles. I liked this bright, weird undersea video and the claustrophobia of the song, about the frustration of waiting for something to change or happen.

The Cure wrote songs about yearning, sadness and most of all love, and they evoked these feelings in a way that was mythical and magical. They had their own alternate reality, with their bird's nest hairdos and lipstick and their strange dress-up videos full of curious things: taxidermy cats and Chinese dragons, giant spiders and blue apples, paddling pools and bear suits. The more I found out about The Cure the more I was drawn into their world. As a teenager Robert Smith had been suspended from school for being an undesirable influence, with his long hair and habit of wearing a floor-length women's fur coat. He would go on to influence millions of people, although there was something about The Cure that made me feel they existed for me alone or, at least, I had a special connection to them. Many of their fans felt this way. Of all teenage musical phases, The Cure is one many of my present-day friends have in their pasts. They too scrutinised the videos and set up Cure shrines in their bedrooms. One friend completed her shrine by converting a giant Swatch wall clock into a Cure clock with a picture of Robert Smith's legs – his hallmark black jeans with puffy white sneakers – on the clock face.

Cure fans had a lot of merchandise to choose from; posters, postcards and T-shirts. I'd wanted the classic *Disintegration* shirt with the picture of the album cover on it: Robert Smith's face floating among flowers printed on a black background. On the day I went to buy my Cure shirt from Virgin Records in Pitt Street Mall, however, there were only white shirts, with the band standing in the snow underneath palm trees, a still from the 'Pictures of You' video clip. I liked the tinkling, wind-chime sound of the song but it wasn't one I would have chosen as a favourite. I bought the shirt anyway. I'd been saving up for quite some time and couldn't bear to go home empty handed.

I debuted the shirt on an outing to a basketball game at the Entertainment Centre with my friend Rachael and the youth group from her family's church. I hated all forms of sport and had grown up in a non-religious household – up until this point I had consistently refused all youth group offers, and I thought it was time to at least try it. I accepted her invitation. Rachael understood me the best of all my friends from school and she, at least, would be on my side.

I thought teenage Christians would be kind, forgiving and gentle but I underestimated the power of hormones; the most important thing was who was in and who was out. Nathan, the guy who seemed to be the most popular member of the youth group, immediately told me my clothes were weird. I was proud. My Cure shirt had been declared a success.

As we sat in the Entertainment Centre, watching the Sydney Kings, my thoughts drifted to what other, older and cooler people were doing elsewhere in the city, and how one day I would be one of them. Of this destiny I was sure. The Cure shirt was the start of my new, different life.

My friend Lynne and I had an arrangement by which we travelled to the city together, first visiting Red Eye Records so I could to look at CDs and vinyl, then Galaxy Bookshop so she could look at science fiction and fantasy books. Although our tastes in books and music were divergent, we shared a brief, intense love of Ratcat. We were two of the many thousands of teenage girls who fell in love with them after seeing 'That Ain't Bad' on *Video Hits*, but being one of many by no means quelled our ardour. We walked into the bushland near my house and stood on the edge of the cliff, singing 'That Ain't Bad' and every other Ratcat song we knew at the top of our lungs, out into the gully. I bought the cassette of the album *Blind Love* immediately upon its release in 1991 and taped a copy for Lynne; she gave me a copy of the *Twin Peaks* soundtrack album in return.

We must have seen the Ratcat shirts on one of our previous city excursions and lobbied our parents for the funds, or in my case probably saved up from money given for more sensible things such as lunch. They were for sale at HMV, a big basement of a store in the middle of Pitt Street Mall. The long-sleeve black shirts had RATCAT written down the sleeves in red. The band's logo, a cartoon rat skull and cat skull, were printed in two big red splotches on the front. I had already copied this design onto the pages of my school diary and onto my pencilcase, which was a palimpsest of musical phases. Every time I'd fall in love with a new band I added their name or their logo on there until they all blended into an unintelligible mess.

After we bought our matching Ratcat shirts the fire alarms began to sound. We looked around confused for a moment, then we along with the rest of the shoppers in the store were bundled out the fire exit, which led us through a tunnel then released us onto George Street. Thrilled by our dramatic exit, we paused to put on our Ratcat shirts then walked out into the city, arm in arm.

My Ned's Atomic Dustbin shirt was my favourite shirt from my early teenage years. An English group best known for having two bass-players and the song 'Kill your Television', Ned's Atomic Dustbin were a cartoon kind of band, dreadlocks, pasty boy legs, and rainbow paint-splattered record covers.

At first I had planned to buy a Welcome Mat shirt. The Welcome Mat were a Sydney band and I'd seen their video for the song '10 000 people with the same idea' on *The Afternoon Show* and liked its lo-fi, shot-in-the-living-room aesthetic. The coveted shirt was white with lots of fluoro text on it, the kind of comments that might be found scratched into the desks of university libraries. It seemed like witty, cynical banter, mysterious and appealing to me as a 13 year old.

Arriving at Waterfront records to purchase the Welcome Mat shirt I discovered I'd come too late: they were sold out. Studying the T-shirts covering the back wall of the shop, the Ned's Atomic Dustbin shirt caught my eye. It was black with GOD FODDER written in large red letters. The 'O' of God was the band's logo, a radiation symbol surrounded by the name and a circle of dynamic ooze.

The shirt made my mother suspicious: was it blasphemous? What did 'God Fodder' mean, anyway? I had no answers for her. If I was honest with myself, I was suspicious about the name too. Was it cool and absurd, or just stupid? The name 'Ned's Atomic Dustbin' came from *The Goon Show*, a radio program which was a favourite of my grandfather. When we lived with my grandparents he would listen to *The Goon Show* every midday on the old radio that lived perennially on the dining room table. As for 'God Fodder', it was the name of the band's first album, and I assumed its significance was the rhythmical sound of the words together.

Most of my musical knowledge at the time came from listening to the radio and reading the street press and British music press like the *NME* and *Melody Maker*. This was how I knew useless details such as how Ned's Atomic Dustbin had got their name and that they, like

The Wonder Stuff and Pop Will Eat Itself, were from a town called Stourbridge in England. The Stourbridge scene was even important enough to warrant a book to be published about it in 1992, *The Eight Legged Atomic Dustbin Will Eat Itself*.

The *NME* often made mention of 'T-shirt bands', of which Ned's Atomic Dustbin was one. They produced a huge variety of T-shirts, possibly more than songs. Most of their shirts were variations on the band's logo; my shirt was one of dozens of different designs. Although I bought the smallest size it was still like wearing a sack and I felt like a small white grub inside it, as if the shirt wore me rather than the other way around. People would read the shirt with looks of confusion; perhaps they thought I was an anti-nuclear Christian.

My Mudhoney shirt combined an unlikely mixture of genres: grunge and cake decorating. It was a white shirt with a colourful, layered cake pictured on it, and on top of the cake were tiny figures with tiny guitars. Those who didn't know who Mudhoney were would compliment me on the cake, but those in the know would, I hoped, register that I was the kind of person to identify with grunge anthems such as 'Touch Me I'm Sick'.

This shirt was responsible for my first love interest. Any attention I had paid to boys up until this time was entirely abstract. I went to an all girls' school and lived with my mother and my sister and the few boys I did encounter – friends' brothers or their church youth group crushes – didn't seem capable of the danger or imagination I regarded as necessary for romance. Music was a perfectly good best friend and boyfriend, and I spent most of my life beyond school sitting in my room listening to the radio and recording songs onto cassettes. Occasionally

I'd accompany my mother to the supermarket just to get out of the house.

On one of these trips I was in the local Franklins with my mother. I was wearing my Mudhoney shirt, black denim shorts and Converse All Stars. As usual I wasn't happy with my appearance, but it would have to do until I could get my ears pierced multiple times and dye my hair unnatural colours. I felt a little less gawky than I had as a 12 year old in a Cure shirt, but at 14 I was still far from satisfied with my look.

'Mudhoney. Cool shirt,' said a guy in a Franklins uniform, who was stacking shelves in one of the aisles. I was shocked that a boy was talking to me – let alone one who liked the same music as me. I blushed and could think of nothing to say in response. I spent so much of my time imagining people like me existed, but then here was someone who at least liked the same music and I was terrified. I opened my mouth and stuttered out a thank you. My mother, amused, observed our awkward conversation.

I was perplexed by the Franklins guy's shorts and long socks, which seemed an oddly elderly look, especially coupled with his scruffy hair, but every time I went to the supermarket I looked for him. The times I managed to go there alone he was never there. His shifts seemed to coincide with the trips I'd make with my mother.

On one of these occasions, he said he had a lot of old band T-shirts that he didn't wear anymore. The Cramps, Violent Femmes ... he might bring them in one day and we could perhaps go down to his car and look at them together.

As exciting as this was, I was terrified by the thought of talking to him alone, in the car park, and never took him up on his offer. It was unclear what the offer involved: was I to buy the shirts? Admire the shirts? Would we kiss? I avoided Franklins for a while and by the time I returned he must have stopped working there as I never saw him again.

The Meanies wrote songs that were short blasts of buzzy pop punk, usually lasting no longer than two minutes. Their songs had names like 'Gangrenous', 'Rambomania' and 'Dr Seuss', and the band did seem like something that could come from a Dr Seuss book, if he had written a book about punks. Although they were from Melbourne they often toured Sydney, and I had an ad for one of their shows stuck on my wall: it was called the 'Ugly As Sin' tour, and there was a reduced price for people who attended wearing paper bags over their heads.

Meanies shirts and album artwork featured illustrations by the singer, Link Meanie. Like The Ramones, who were their obvious inspiration, all of them had the band name as their surname. When they played live, Link – a tall, skinny guy with long brown dreadlocks – would throw himself around the stage as if he was indestructible.

I saw the Meanies shirt hanging up on the wall at Half A Cow, a tiny book and record store on Glebe Point Road. Before I bought it I asked the man working there what he thought the picture on it was. It was a highly detailed illustration with things that could have been faces, or could have been machines. 'I dunno,' he said, and I handed over my $20 for the shirt, satisfied it was an abstract illustration and not something I was too young to know about.

Although I was a bit more confident than I had been in the days of my failed Franklins romance a year earlier, I still had to gather up courage before I approached the counter in record stores. The people who worked there had positions of great prestige. Approaching them with a question about a T-shirt or CD was almost as nerve-wracking as asking someone on a date, which I could only imagine, as I had never done that.

At home I dragged out the heavy sewing machine to make the shirt smaller. I was glad of the years of compulsory school sewing lessons as I effortlessly completed one of home economics' greatest challenges:

threading the sewing machine. My plan was to convert the Meanies shirt from a sack suitable for a large, broad-shouldered man to something a bit more flattering. I cut the excess length away and sewed in the sides. Even though this method never quite worked as expertly as I hoped it would, I looked a bit less lost inside it.

Wearing my new Meanies

shirt I felt like I had an extra layer of protection, a spiky kind of armour. I made sure to wear it to school on the one day of the year students were allowed to wear their own clothes rather than the unbecoming tartan uniform. A lot of thought and preparation went into Mufti Day, the day we revealed our true identities. Occasionally, a rebel or innovator would make a statement. A girl in the year below mine wore only a blanket with a hole cut in it for her head. No one spoke of anything else for quite some time afterwards. My boots, Meanies shirt and tie-dye slip seemed suddenly boring by comparison.

I wore all of my band T-shirts until they fell apart and most didn't make it beyond the 1990s. Although I don't remember discarding them I no longer own them, and the time is long past since band T-shirts were my default outfit. The only people who wear them consistently these days are heavy-metal fans who still wear long sleeve black shirts with hideous graphics on the front as they have done since the 80s and will until the end of time. Certain iconic designs have stuck around too, like the Joy Division *Unknown Pleasures* album cover, now also available in shoe, tote bag and G-string form. Other shirts in this 'iconic' category are The Ramones logo or the Misfits skull face but these are worn more as symbols than to show love for the music.

Just because people don't wear them much, doesn't mean they haven't kept them, as I realise when I go to see a 90s band playing a reunion

show. In this space safe for nostalgia people bring their shirts out again. At a Hummingbirds reunion show I lined up at the bar behind a guy in a Carter USM shirt. Carter were an English duo, two guys called Jim Bob and Fruitbat, who played fuzzy punk guitar over samples and drum machines. They had a moment of notoriety in 1991 when their song 'After the Watershed' included the line 'Goodbye Ruby Tuesday' and they were sued by The Rolling Stones. After the scandal I had forgotten about Jim Bob and Fruitbat, although others evidently had not.

Then outside I spotted one of my friends wearing a Hummingbirds shirt that he'd kept since the early 90s, with the band's name and a picture of a hummingbird on it. The shirt had once come as a free gift with a seven-inch single. We'd been chatting for a while when a man wearing an identical Hummingbirds shirt came up to us. 'Is it ... from the time?' he asked, daring to hope that he was not the only one.

Generation X

One night while waiting for *Rage* to start I was watching *Eat Carpet*, the short film program on SBS. *Eat Carpet* showed anything from ten minutes of impressionist squiggles to mind-bending claymation universes, to mockumentaries about bogan culture in the Blue Mountains. One night it showed a film called *Close Personal Friend*, an interview with the Canadian author Douglas Coupland.

Coupland spoke about being alive but not having a life, inspired by the expression 'get a life'. He spoke about archaeologists of the future digging up California and finding endless fitness centres and wondering at a culture so obsessed with torture; how technology is changing our perception of time; and the moment in cartoons in which a character takes a black circle of fabric out of their pocket, puts it on the ground, and escapes through it. Through the hole, Coupland said, was the future. At the end of the interview he urged us to jump into it.

I would have followed him into the hole. There was something compellingly smart about this neat, suited man, swivelling in an Eames chair, talking about the past and the future as if both were as within our grasp as the present.

I borrowed Coupland's book, *Generation X,* from the library. As well as the story, which was based around three friends who live in Palm Springs and drive to ruined landscapes to tell each other fables, the sidebars of the pages included terms and their definitions. Many of them were to do with low pay, low prestige jobs, or, as Coupland called them,

McJobs. As well as the glossary there were Jenny Holzer-like slogans:

NOSTALGIA IS A WEAPON.

USE JETS WHILE YOU STILL CAN.

YOU MIGHT NOT COUNT IN THE NEW ORDER.

My favourite slogan was WE'RE BEHAVING LIKE INSECTS, which I painted onto a T-shirt, writing the words in capital letters with white fabric paint. Wearing it I felt as if I couldn't be fooled by anything. My other favourite saying – 'How Odd' – I had engraved onto a round, purple aluminium pet tag at Mister Minit. I wore the tag as a necklace, and wearing both slogans I felt as if I was charmed, ready to jump through the black hole.

Compared to the characters in the novel my life had barely begun. Andrew, Dag and Claire were in their 20s and lived in a bittersweet, 20th Century fable of toxic waste and flocks of doves, cosmetic surgery and palm trees, dead celebrities and childhood memories. Everything around them and everything that had happened to them was filtered into their interweaving stories. Even though the characters' lives had little resonance with mine I liked this idea, that life could be thought of as a story.

NINETY 9 | 23

When I was a child I spent a lot of time creating stories about my alter ego, whom I named Laura Appleyard. She lived in an orphanage and had a secret identity as a fortune-telling gypsy girl. I'd lie in bed at night and devise new Laura Appleyard adventures until I fell asleep. I'd retained this habit, although I no longer told myself stories about orphans and gypsies. Now when I lay in bed at night I told myself stories about my future self. I'd first imagine my basement apartment on a city street corner, inside which everything was red or black, and then move onto my clothes, lots of lace and ribbons and silver jewellery, and then to my paintings, as I was destined to be an artist. I'd imagine all this in such detail that usually I'd fall asleep before my future self had a chance to do anything but look around her black and red den, with its lava lamps and four-poster bed.

All thoughts of my future life came up against the same obstacle. It appeared at the end of *Generation X* also – the last chapter was titled 'Jan. 01, 2000'. Looking at all those zeroes made me feel uneasy, like they might wipe out everything that came before them. I would be 21 years old by the time everything was reset. It was far enough away to be abstract, but close enough to be an endless source of speculation. My worst case scenario for January 1st, 2000 was a ruined landscape much like the cover of the Midnight Oil album *Red Sails in the Sunset*, Sydney Harbour dry and cratered after a nuclear attack and the city in ruins. The future could be an ominous place, even with Douglas Coupland to guide me.

Radio Mix Tape

Every time I move house I faithfully transport my many boxes of cassette tapes. I rarely listen to these cassettes but I can't bring myself to discard them. Inside the boxes they are mixed together in no particular order, cassingles, albums, cassettes that came with fanzines, op-shop purchases and the mix tapes I made from the radio in the 1990s.

In the early 1990s we didn't own a CD player and the record player was a precision machine that I was forbidden to unpack from the boxes in the spare room. Cassettes suited me. I liked that you could make them yourself, compiling the songs and decorating the covers. The covers of my radio mix tapes were embellished with designs I'd drawn in black felt-tip pen, then coloured over with highlighter, each a different colour so I could identify them at a glance as I looked along their spines.

My cassettes were reverently and neatly arranged by my bedside. Here I had a small set of wooden shelves which I had painted with the emblems of a teenage surrealist: a kaleidoscope of cartoon umbrellas, hearts, suns and castles surrounded by yellow and black spirals. On top of the shelves was the JVC double cassette player. I developed a great affinity with this machine and spent many hours perched beside it, recording songs from the radio.

Although mixtapes are often conceived of as gifts or romantic gestures, the ones I most treasured were the radio tapes I made for myself and listened to alone in my room. Whenever I was at home by myself I'd turn them up as loudly as possible and fill the house with music: Beasts of Bourbon, X-Ray Spex, Jane's Addiction, Fugazi, PJ Harvey, Screamfeeder, Dead Kennedys, Babes in Toyland. The tapes were a mix of genres with only one thing in common, that the songs cleared out my head and lifted me out of myself.

I compiled my radio mix tapes carefully. They were a musical education as important as the more conventional education I received at school. A serious student, year after year I was labelled 'quiet and conscientious' on my school reports. This description appeared with such frequency that I imagined myself to be a kind of mole, quietly digging my way through Henry the VIIIth's England, algebra, contour lines, ionic column identification and all the other fragments of information that went into the creation of a well-educated teenager.

I approached my musical education with equal, if not more, vigour: reading music magazines, watching *Rage* and *The Noise* and listening to the radio. I divided my listening time between Triple J and local community radio. There were many small stations hidden along the FM band and I'd go in search of them, slowly inching the tuner dial from one end to the other. I'd been doing this from the days before I was a music fan. When I was a child my father, who would often concoct tall stories about everyday things, had convinced me that voices speaking in languages other than English on our AM/FM radio were actual broadcasts from far away countries, and I'd explore the dial in search of them. The hiss of static was an ocean I travelled.

My radio mix tapes kept me company as I stayed up late drawing or reading, the light from my room one of the few in our street still shining after midnight. I would draw psychedelic versions of Munch's *The Scream* while listening to obscure songs I'd taped from community radio shows, like 'The Cicadas That Ate Five Dock' by Outline about a giant insect attack on the Sydney suburb, or 'Mohawk Man' by Mr Epp and the Calculations, a deadpan takedown of cookie-cutter punks intoned over guitar feedback. Whenever I listened to such songs I wondered if I was the only person in the world listening to them at that exact moment.

The mixes are layers of obscurities, anthems, indie one-hit wonders, classics and lots of songs by The Cure. The Cure's back catalogue included music for all moods, from 'Faith', my despair soundtrack of choice, to the weird disco of 'The Walk', which sounded like elevator music from an alternate universe. One of my oldest radio mix tapes starts with the song 'Hot Hot Hot', in which The Cure do their best impression of a funk band. I struggled to embrace the band's occasional forays into unfamiliar genres, but I wanted to understand them, and so would listen to the song as if it were a bitter, but necessary, vitamin.

A poster was blu-tacked inside an alcove in my bedroom, surrounded by glow-in-the-dark stars, a decorating feature that was at the apex of popularity in the early 1990s. The image on the poster was Robert Smith sitting staring with a look of staged foreboding, as the walls of a tiny living room enclose him. This image was my equivalent of an ancestral portrait; I imagined Smith as a lipstick-wearing uncle who was there for me in times of crisis.

The tape that begins with 'Hot Hot Hot' is a 90-minute Akai cassette with the songs written out on the cardboard insert. The song names are written over the pencil impressions of the songs I recorded them over. At first I had only a limited number of cassettes and as my tastes changed I'd sacrifice music I'd grown out of to my newest discoveries. I was conscious that I had a lot of catching up to do, and so my tapes featured punk classics – 'Another Girl, Another Planet', 'Search and Destroy', 'London Calling' – as well as more forgettable curiosities like 'I Wish You Were a Beer' by the Cycle Sluts from Hell. This snarly pastiche of a heavy metal song had an accompanying video in which the women in the band wore tight leather and thrashed their long hair around. I was pretty sure it wasn't serious but couldn't quite tell.

The tape includes songs by some of the British bands who were popular at the time, The Stone Roses, Teenage Fanclub, Suede and Carter USM. I read a lot about such bands in the *NME* and *Melody Maker*, copies of which would appear at the local newsagent months after their English publication. From reading them I imagined England as a place where everyone communicated in droll repartee. In the English music press deities such as Morrissey and Mark E. Smith were equally revered and ridiculed. The highlight of the *NME* year was the Glastonbury music festival, a romp through muddy fields to the sounds of Primal Scream or Ozric Tentacles. While most of the popular British bands were played on the radio, some of the secondary ones I read about I had little chance of hearing and could only imagine from their names. I would read reviews of Half Man Half Biscuit or The Family Cat, and try to imagine what they might sound like.

By the early 1990s Triple J had changed from being a local Sydney station to a national one, in the process culling most of its staff and causing a great deal of discontent among its Sydney listeners. Demonstrations were held outside the ABC radio offices protesting the sackings and the station's new direction. Demonstrations continued into the 90s. One of them was triggered by the repetitive programming of 1992's 'Endless Summer'. It was renamed by the demonstration organisers as the 'Endless Bummer' on a poster that listed the '5 Deadly Sins of JJJ' accompanied by a photograph of eccentric indie pop anti-hero Lawrence, of the English band Felt.

I hadn't listened to Triple J prior to its nationalisation, and so didn't know what had been lost. The Triple J I knew had a general playlist of alternative rock, and while it could get repetitive, it was still far preferable to listening to The Angels on Triple M, or Girlfriend on 2DayFM, the other two major radio stations. Triple J still played unlikely combinations of artists, mixing up Australian bands with British shoegaze, American grunge, and the occasional dance or electronic track. The novelty romp 'The Size of a Cow' by The Wonder Stuff could be followed up by the snarling seriousness of 'Youth Against Fascism' by Sonic Youth, a Hawaiian surf inspired instrumental by The Cruel Sea, or a serious ballad like the mournful 'Tomorrow Wendy' by Andy Prieboy.

One week in 1991, the Teenage Fanclub album *Bandwagonesque* was the feature album on Triple J. I had made it my personal mission to wait by the radio and record every song from the album, and therefore save myself the expense of buying it. A well-timed Brashs voucher arrived in the mail that week, saving me from this miserly task. I'd won the voucher from having a letter published in *Smash Hits*, a monthly music and celebrity magazine. As children, my sister and I had developed a no-fail formula for winning the colouring-in competitions in the comics section of the Sunday newspapers: go beyond the expected, use glitter. I applied a similar logic of extremity to the *Smash Hits* letters page, and wrote a silly letter about Elvis sightings in suburban Sydney, inspired by the Mojo Nixon song 'Elvis is Everywhere', a psychobilly rant about the ubiquity of the King. This was enough to win the voucher and a badge picturing Blacky, the sock puppet mascot of the letters page. I still have

A DATE N.R.	□ IN □ OUT	B DATE N.R.	□ IN □ OUT

The Cure - Hot Hot Hot.   Cure - Faith
Teenage Fanclub-God knows.   4 7 8 1
Soulscraper-heard it all before Nick Cave-Weeping Song
Carter USM-After the Watershed Mudhoney - ?
Only Ones- Another Girl. Cycle Sluts from
Stone Roses-I wanna be. Hell-I wish you were
Splash-splash   . a beer—
Stooges-Search & Destroy. Therapy- Teethgrinder
Lemonheads-being around. NAD-Walking in Syrup
The Clash - London Calling. Lemonheads - Luca
boys next door-shivers   " Different Drum

this badge. It has the appearance of the kind of obscure object I might find at a flea market, except this time I know its story.

The Brashs store on Pitt Street included the piano showroom to which our family had made numerous visits prior to purchasing the upright Steinberg which resided in our living room. The cultural environment in my home was one in which classical music was encouraged and anything else treated with extreme suspicion. Listening to pop or rock felt like an act of rebellion, and the louder and angrier, the greater the transgression. But it was this forbidden music that meant something to me, even though my mother described it as unintelligent 'bang bang' music or 'dirge music'. I was forever being asked to turn it down. By the end of 1991 I had given up piano and cello lessons and hired a red bass guitar from the school music department. I played along to Cure and Ramones songs, and tried to think up band names that hadn't been already taken, for my non-existent band of one girl and her hired bass guitar.

Music had become a central, lifesaving force for me, but it was one I mostly experienced alone. I felt like the songs I loved were spells that only worked on me, although I did have Rachael as an ally and I tried to convert my other school friends to the music I liked. I carefully prepared mix tapes for them, cutting out inserts from cardboard and decorating the covers. Rachael and I collaborated on a tape called 'Sid ate ABBA for Breakfast (then spewed them back up again)', referring to Sid Vicious and our disgust at the current wave of nostalgia for ABBA after the release of *ABBA Gold* in 1992. While my friends weren't entirely disinterested in such attempts, the tapes never had their desired effect.

Whenever I felt particularly lonely I extracted my diary from its hiding spot underneath my bedside table. I had converted an address book with a green marbled cover for this purpose. Hammering a nail through one side I made a hole through which I affixed a padlock, to deter would-be readers. Inside I wrote in tiny, angry script about feeling trapped, in my body, in the suburbs, and in my life.

Sometimes Triple J would play a Henry Rollins spoken-word piece called 'I Know You', a portrait of an outsider, the subject of ridicule, who could only ever know comfort from wrapping their arms around themself to imagine someone holding them. My diary contained similar sentiments, but the thought that loneliness was a common affliction shared by many horrified, rather than comforted, me. I feared this feeling would persist throughout my entire life and, like the Rollins protagonist, I would end up with solitude as my only reliable ally.

Music was my most powerful antidote to loneliness. Triple J was a good fallback option but the highlights of my week were listening to particular community radio shows. They were secrets, hidden among the static of the dial and among the other programs on local stations, which could vary from original 1930s swing radio broadcasts, ambient electronica, or request shows for prisoners. I never knew what I might hear, especially late at night when the graveyard-shift programs were on. It seemed that pretty much anyone could get a show on community radio if they could work the equipment and were reliable enough to turn up for their show every week.

On community radio, presenters could be as idiosyncratic and keep as loose a reign over their shows as they liked. I delighted in the technical glitches, patches of dead air and their occasional – or frequent, depending on the presenter – rants and personal stories. These shows were good company on school nights, like having a friend with an excellent music collection come to visit. Here and there between songs on my mix tapes are the voices of community radio presenters, each instantly recognisable to me even now.

One tape begins with the voice of Wayne DZ announcing a Sonic Youth cover of the one hit wonder 'Ca Plane Pour Moi', originally by Plastic Bertrand. Wayne DZ presented a program on 2SER called *The Alternative Music Show* and the occasional track by well-known bands like Sonic Youth aside, mostly he played obscure punk and 60s garage seven-inch singles. I'd discovered the show one night while floating along the FM band, past the tight cluster of commercial stations and up towards the very top end of the FM dial. The songs had rough edges, they crackled and sparked out of the speakers. I felt that if this kind of music was my soundtrack, I was automatically part of a cool, underground world, just by listening to it.

As well as the music, I enjoyed a growing sense of familiarity with the show and its listeners, for whom occasional requests would be played. My favourite *Alternative Music Show* listener was a punk guy who worked as as a school bus driver. I imagined a bus blaring the Newtown Neurotics or Psychotic Turnbuckles, with kids hanging out the windows giving the finger to the cars passing by.

Most of the bands played on *The Alternative Music Show* I hadn't heard before so I set about my study of it conscientiously, writing down the songs played and recording a rating for each using a code of circles and dashes. A dash indicated indifference, a circle mild dislike, a coloured-in circle strong dislike. A tick indicated approval and a circled tick indicated strong approval, an honour reserved for tape-worthy songs like 'Over Now' by The Eastern Dark, a song with a dark, crashing sense of finality, or 'Fun' by The Thought Criminals, a song about eschewing musical fame for the fun of being in a punk band, getting drunk, and wearing rags and garbage bags.

As well as the regular shows I listened to I'd often browse the dial. The graveyard-shift programs, which covered the night hours from 1am to 6am, played unusual ambient music, or slow and growling death metal, or featured people having long, rambling conversations about the nature of existence. I could rarely stay up that late but if I found a particularly weird or interesting show I'd put in a tape, press record, turn the sound down and go to sleep. The click of the tape switching off only woke me momentarily, and in the morning I'd have a have a tape full of strange recordings.

I put a lot of effort into my radio mix tapes, with the aim of making them as seamless as possible. The songs I taped would often be missing the first ten or 20 seconds as I waited for the presenter to stop speaking, or rushed to cue up the tape in the right place. My finger would hover over the pause button, waiting for the perfect moment to start recording. These versions, with my DIY editing, became the versions I knew. If I heard the same songs in full elsewhere they didn't sound quite right, the same feeling as having a dream in which I discover an extra room in my house.

Listening to these tapes now, rather than the songs it is the squeaks and pops of the stops and pauses between songs, the scraps of voices, and the flashes of other, taped-over songs that are interesting to me. In these sounds I can imagine my touch on the buttons of the cassette player. I like to believe that in these instants on the tape something of that time has been captured, an ambience, the ghost of my past, teenage self.

Request Show

A number of community radio shows were request shows. The first program I called in for a request to was *Contact*. It broadcast on a station which was at the very start of the dial, 2RDJ, and required full extension of the aerial and a steady hand in order to tune into it. I had a fear of making phone calls and had listened to request shows for years, too shy to call up. On the night of my first request my mother and sister were at a piano concert and I was alone in the house. I had eaten my way through some mini Violet Crumbles and was feeling a sugary sense of bravery. I called and immediately made the mistake of requesting 'I Know it's Over' by The Smiths. 'Oh no!' Andrew, the show's presenter, said. 'Look, people are always ringing up for "I Know It's Over" and I'm sick of it!' One of the more maudlin of Smiths songs, it opens with the line 'Mother, I can feel the soil falling over my head', before unfurling as a morbid melodrama that I believed appealed to me alone. I was genuinely surprised that other people liked it too, while being embarrassed that my choice was so predictable.

Another request radio show I listened to regularly was *The R Zone*, which broadcast late on Saturday nights. I tried a different request tactic for this show. As well as encouraging people to call the phone number, the presenter, Matt, sometimes gave out the postal address of the station. Feeling more confident with print than the phone, I wrote a letter, requesting the song 'Fish Heads' by Barnes and Barnes. For all my adoration of serious, reflective lyrics, I also had a liking for novelty songs.

My interest in novelty songs had been inspired by 'Where's Me Jumper' by the Sultans of Ping FC, an indie hit in the UK in 1992 which made it onto the Triple J playlist. Silly as it was, this song was rather a revelation to me. I felt inspired by the fact that you *could* write a song about losing a jumper at a disco and it would be played on the radio on the other side of the world. Such songs were a welcome counterbalance to the seriousness of grunge whenever they were played on Triple J and there were plenty of them, the deadpan 'Detachable Penis' by King Missile, or the falsetto, karaoke-hell cover of 'Wuthering Heights' by Melbourne band Mr Floppy, from their album *The Unbearable Lightness of Being a Dickhead*.

I posted my letter and on the show that week Matt played 'Fish Heads' for 'Vanessa of Turramurra'. I was proud to join the ranks of other requesters, identified by their name and suburb, regulars such as Daniel of Concord West, or Elaine of Beecroft. I liked to imagine these northern suburbs people listening to the radio in their rooms. Matt had seemed amused by my letter and so I continued to write, each week requesting another song. One week I decided I would call him up instead. I dragged the phone into my room and sat leaning against the door, gathering my courage. It was after midnight and my mother and sister had long since retreated to bed. Nervous that I might wake them, I dialed the number of the radio station.

Matt and I talked for a long time, despite my worries I was clogging up the request line. Mostly we talked about music. Record stores, favourite videos played on *Rage,* new albums, our musical idols. We got on so well that I called every week at 12:30 and we'd have long conversations. I did my best to talk about interesting topics, aware that he was older than me and Year Ten anecdotes were not going to interest him. Sometimes, though, I'd relate the more bizarre episodes of high school life, such as the day we were rounded up and marched to the library to watch a video about the dangers of graffiting trains, in which a spray-painting young man fell to his death to the soundtrack of 'Run to Paradise' by the Choirboys.

One night on the phone we conspired to meet up after the show had finished. We'd had so many phone conversations, and I'd listened to his show for so long, that I was curious to meet the person behind the voice. I changed into a Pixies T-shirt and turned my attention to my bedroom window. My room was at the back of the house and faced onto the garden. Underneath the window was a concrete path and the dog-house where Billy the Golden Retriever resided. As I squeezed through the window and dropped down to the path below, the dog watched curiously. Delighted to have a visitor in the middle of the night, Billy's tail wagged frantically as I tiptoed to the side gate. 'Good boy,' I whispered, 'no barking'.

I slipped out the gate and past the Ford Telstar in the carport, and padded down the driveway, carrying my boots. The street was still as a painting, so dark and quiet I could easily imagine the world had stopped. I sat against the fence and in a little while a set of headlights appeared at the end of the street and slowly came closer.

Matt's car had the numberplate LIZ.

'Is that your car's name?' I asked, after he had stopped and got out of the car to greet me.

'No, it's my mother's car,' he said. It was strange to hear his voice coming from a person, rather than a radio. He was very tall, a kind of boy-giant with a friendly round face and long brown hair. He wore a red flannelette shirt over a Sub Pop T-shirt with 'Loser' written across the chest, and trousers tucked into black army boots.

I too was wearing boots, the eight-hole Dr Martens which I'd persuaded my mother to buy for me the previous Christmas. We compared boots for a moment, as I nervously glanced back towards the windows of my house. Of all the disobedient things I'd done in my life, this was going to a new level. But it was an adventure, and I wanted to prolong it. We decided to go for a drive.

The car was messy with empty soft drink bottles and cassette cases, and the many crates of CDs Matt played on his radio show were stacked in the back. We drove around Turramurra aimlessly, listening to the tape he had made of his show from earlier that night. 'New World

Order' by Ministry, 'Repulsion' by Dinosaur Jr., 'Def Con One' by Pop Will Eat Itself. Where should we go? 'I'll show you the radio station,' he decided.

I felt happy travelling through the night suburbs, watching the near-empty streets out the window, enjoying the feeling of being awake and moving through the world while most others slept. The radio station was in a little cottage on Victoria Road, at the edge of the Gladesville Hospital. It wasn't what I imagined a radio station to be like, it looked more like a house one's grandparents might live in. The two radio studios were compact rooms with soundproofed doors at the back of the cottage. A pre-recorded overnight show was playing and Matt explained how they were recorded on VHS tape, so they could run for eight hours continuously. I felt as if I were snooping in a stranger's house as I peeked in at the panel with its lights and buttons, read the messages on the noticeboard and the names on the pigeon-holes where my letter must have arrived for Matt months before.

After leaving the station we stopped off at an all night convenience store where one of Matt's friends worked. This guy had long hair and wore a death metal band T-shirt, and we chatted to him as we microwaved pink iced donuts to the point of gooiness. 'Yeah,' he sighed, 'it's a pretty quiet night in Chatswood West.'

Outside the store we stood under the glare of the fluorescent lights, trying to decide where to go next.

'Let's drive through Kings Cross,' Matt said.

In the 1990s Kings Cross had yet to be gentrified and everything I knew about it came from stories of vice and drugs reported on the nightly news, so I was curious to see the real place from inside the safety of the car.

We drove over the Harbour Bridge, then turned up William Street. The red bars of the Coca Cola sign flashed and blinked at the top of the hill. The main street of the Cross was bright with lights and signs and the streets were busy, even though it was 3am. On Victoria Street I watched out the car window as touts enticed groups of men into strip clubs, and people hung around in groups on the street, smoking. Women in tiny skirts and high heels, men with ruined faces, groups of drunk guys from the suburbs.

I watched the scene outside as if it were a movie running past the windows, gathering all the details. This was another part of Sydney to add to my ever-expanding atlas. At the end of the neon-lit street we drove down the hill to Woolloomooloo, then back towards the Harbour Bridge and along the highway to Turramurra. My street was as dark and silent as it had been when we left it.

'I'll call you on your show next week,' I said, and watched the car disappear up the street before sitting down on the gutter to unlace my boots. I took them off and tiptoed up the driveway, through the gate and climbed back through the window into my room.

Cassingle

Of all the formats available for songs in the 90s, cassingles were the cheapest and least prestigious. Cassingles seemed almost disposable, in their cardboard sleeves, wrapped in plastic film with a pull tab like a packet of cigarettes. Most had only two songs on them, the single and the B-side, which was usually a dark horse I tried my best to like. The tape would start and finish with an arpeggio of bleeps, a toneburst that bookended the songs.

As a listening experience cassingles were almost over before they began, but that brief period of time was like opening a door into a different atmosphere. 'High' by The Cure was a twinkling, dreamlike place, a flying dream. 'Black Bandages' by the Falling Joys was a dervish of guitar fuzz, both hard and gentle. Others, like singles by Pearl Jam or the Candy Harlots, I bought because they were 99 cents. If I decided I didn't like the song I stuck tape over the holes on the top of the cassette and used them to record songs that I preferred.

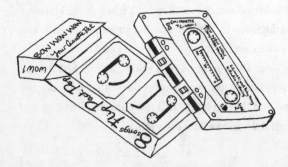

Sydney Record Stores

The first record stores I visited regularly were those embedded in suburban shopping malls, like Angel Music in the Macquarie Centre. This small store mostly sold whatever was in the charts, be it John Farnham or Def FX, and it was here I'd browse cassingles and pick up copies of the street press newspapers. I then returned to the ice rink at the back of the shopping centre and sat on the cold, rink-side seats while my sister skated. I would read every word of the *Drum Media* and *On the Street*, from the letters page at the beginning to the classified ads for musicians wanted at the end. The highlight of every skating session was when the ice rink musak played 'Rock 'n' Roll High School' by The Ramones. It had somehow slipped onto the playlist, which was mostly late 80s chart hits like 'Infinity' by Guru Josh.

Angel Music had its limitations. One day I asked if they had the album *Ritual de lo Habitual* by Jane's Addiction. I stumbled over its tongue twister name and, after being told they didn't have it, I fled the store in embarrassment. The album cover art featured a nude sculpture and had been declared obscene by some music stores in America; I wondered whether this was why they didn't stock it. Maybe there wasn't enough demand for Jane's Addiction in North Ryde. I would have to look elsewhere.

I discovered the existence of Waterfront Records in the pages of the *Drum Media*. Waterfront's handwritten ads were printed alongside the gig guide and included information about what was new instore as well as the strangest UFO and freaks-of-nature stories culled from the *Weekly World News*. I worked out a plan to visit it, looking up the address in our street directory, a book so old that whole suburbs had been built in the time since it was printed.

One of my tasks as a big sister was to escort Fiona to choir practice on Saturday mornings. She sung in a choir affiliated with the Sydney Opera Company and practice sessions were held at the Opera Centre on Elizabeth Street in Surry Hills. I was instructed on no account to leave the building, as it was surrounded by danger: drug addicts, criminals, and persons of ill repute. As soon as practise started, I slipped out the door and went exploring.

If I walked fast, I could make it to Waterfront and back within the first session of choir practice and no one would notice I was gone. Waterfront was a small store on Barlow St, off George Street near Central station. I liked to imagine that Barlow Lane had been named after Lou Barlow from the lo-fi band Sebadoh. It was an unassuming laneway slipped in beside a 70s high rise: the McKell Building which no one ever seemed to enter or leave.

Inside the store every inch of space was used. The shop windows were lined with LPs and the back wall was covered with a display of band T-shirts. This was the section that interested me the most and I would lie in bed at night and imagine having my pick of anything I wanted from the T-shirt wall. In real life approaching the counter at

Waterfront was a nerve-wracking experience. I felt like a tiny mouse as I imagined the cool, inner-city lives of the people who worked there, my voice coming out as a squeak.

One day, during a Sex Pistols phase, I picked out a copy of *Sid Sings*, the Sid Vicious solo album. *Sid Sings* is one of the worst albums I own, a muddy live recording of a New York gig at Max's Kansas City in 1978. When I bought it, the man behind the counter said, 'I was at that show.'

'Really?' was all I managed to splutter.

When I listened to *Sid Sings* I imagined the Waterfront guy in the audience. My favourite part of it was the heckling in between songs.

'You wanna do it my way arseholes?' Vicious slurs by way of introducing his version of 'My Way'. There is a lull as the song starts up.

'You're a poser!' a woman heckles, her voice clear and wise.

I listened to this small segment of the album on repeat, imagining the heckler to look a bit like Deborah Harry, with silvery blonde hair and sharp features, wearing a striped shirt and tight black jeans.

My early days of illicit Waterfront visits ceased when I discovered other record stores and Waterfront moved to a larger space on York Street, near the Queen Victoria Building. I'd travel into the city to go on a record-store crawl, beginning with either Waterfront or Red Eye, the store with the round, bloodshot eye as its logo. The eye made me think of the kind of people who wore all black at all times and stayed up all night watching B-grade movies and listening to The Cramps. Red Eye Records was in the Tank Stream Arcade, a subterranean arcade at the northern end of Pitt Street Mall. The arcade was a calm place, dimly-lit with tiled walls, and hidden beneath it ran the Tank Stream after which it was named.

The walls of Red Eye were painted red and gave me the feeling I was in the belly of a large, music-eating monster. Beside the store there was a food court with 70s-orange plastic seats, where sometimes Lynne and I would sit and watch people going in and out of Red Eye. People would leave the store holding bags with the logo on them and sometimes in the above ground world I would catch glimpses of these eyes among the legs of city crowds. Bags from music stores were like symbols for a secret club. The Waterfront plastic bag was white with a yellow and black Sydney cityscape on it and when I caught sight of it, or a Red Eye bag, I'd feel a sense of kinship with whoever carried it.

In Red Eye, as well as Waterfront, I could make contact with the objects that matched the music I heard on the radio. I could examine *Loveless* by My Bloody Valentine, which had a saturated pink, multiple exposure photograph of a guitar on the cover, or the Clouds' *Loot* EP, the cover for which seemed to be a pattern of curved mirrors until I looked closely and saw they were the foil balloons from wine casks, inflated into pillows. Even if I didn't buy anything it was the strangeness of the store – with its big bloodshot eye logo and the posters for bands I'd never heard of – that I came to absorb.

Despite the records being mostly out of my price range, there was a magazine section with fanzines for sale for one or two dollars. This was where I discovered zines and they thrilled me with their slapdash weirdness. There were music fanzines like *Lemon*, a Sydney zine comprised of an extroverted collection of interviews, music reviews and rants. It became notorious in early 1993 when the editor, Louise Dickinson, wrote an inflammatory review of the anodyne folk duo Club Hoy, suggesting they deserved 'a good raping'. The scandal spread from the underground to mainstream media, even appearing as the subject of a segment on *A Current Affair*. I followed reports of the scandal, worried about what effect mainstream scrutiny would have on this underground world I so wanted to be a part of. The controversy settled, but *Lemon* continued for only a short time afterwards, as Dickinson died in 1995. I read about her overdose death in the street press, in the same way I found out about other untimely deaths in the Sydney music scene, Goose from Box the Jesuit, Stevie of The Plunderers. I would feel a sense of displaced sadness even if I had known little about them previously.

Another store in the Tank Stream Arcade was a smaller branch of Red Eye which sold secondhand records and CDs, as well as posters. I bought my poster of Robert Smith here and, finding myself short of the $8 needed to by it, offered them a postage stamp to make up the difference. I wanted the poster so much I was willing to bear the shame. They refused the stamp and let me have it for 40 cents less, probably feeling sorry for me.

Further south towards Central station and next on the record store trail was Phantom records. Phantom was on Pitt Street, under the tracks of the monorail and near the vast hole in the ground on the corner of Liverpool Street, once Anthony Horden department store, and destined to become World Square. Painted on the window of Phantom records was the Phantom-comic-inspired slogan 'the big beat in the heart of the vinyl jungle.' I liked the sound of this but it didn't fit with my perception of Phantom records, which was a jungle of scruffy guitar players. As with Red Eye and Waterfront, Phantom was also a record label – multiple copies of their releases could often been found on the shelves – Crow's *Sunburnt Throats and Happy Thunderclouds* on brown vinyl or the 'Passenger Blues'

seven-inch single by The Deadly Hume, with the angry, cryptic cover art of two boys facing-off on a railway track.

Phantom seemed more DIY than Waterfront or Red Eye, it was the place to buy demo cassettes and scratchy punk zines, and felt less like a shop and more like a living room well stocked with records. When I saw the Sydney punk band Lawnsmell play an in-store at Phantom it did seem rather like I was at a show in someone's house, people crammed into a space designed for much quieter activities. Lawnsmell played a screamy punk cover of 'Birthday' by the Sugarcubes which thrilled me, as well as my favourite song of theirs, 'My T-shirt', which went for about 20 seconds and had only one line: 'My T-shirt smells like dirt'.

A block down from Phantom, across the road from the big hole in the ground, was a row of secondhand record stores, Ashwoods, Lawsons and The Pitt. Of these it was Ashwoods where I spent the most time browsing. It was a Sydney institution and had already been operating for 60 years by the time I discovered it. The store had a spiral staircase leading up to a mezzanine upper level where magazines and comics were sold, but most of the action happened downstairs among the thousands of LPs, grouped only in basic categories. 'Female Vocal' could be mean anything from Frida Boccara to Dolly Parton or Nina Hagen, padded out with hundreds of unknown obscurities.

There were so many records in Ashwoods that I had the feeling anything I was looking for must be in there somewhere, among the Herb Alpert records and 70s pop compilations with names like *Ripper '76* and *Scorcher*. This feeling led to hours spent flipping through the LPs, which were displayed in three levels of bins. Only the bravest risked being trampled by other record collectors to delve into the lowest level, where the dustiest records were kept, hoping to find a treasure no one had yet discovered, or one that someone had hidden down there. Ashwoods had a busy, intense atmosphere and I took pride in taking my place among the serious record-collecting men who flipped through records with maximum efficiency.

Millions of records have come and gone through Ashwoods and records with their distinctive, round-edged price stickers regularly turn up in markets and op-shops. To avoid price switching the price was also marked in pencil on the record's label, another telltale sign of an Ashwoods record. Other stores had their own price sticker idiosyncrasies: Red Eye prices always ended in .98, and Waterfront were known for handwriting descriptions of albums in texta on Post-it notes and affixing them to the covers.

Ashwoods' neighbours were similarly serious record browsing dens: The Pitt, Lawsons, and Martins on the corner of Pitt and Goulburn streets. After a full session of browsing all these stores I'd come up blinking against the bright light of the outside world, my fingers dirty from flipping through dusty records. This end of Pitt Street had other curious businesses, like the Leung Wai Kee Buddhist Craft and Joss Stick Trading Pty Ltd, which sold household objects made out of paper for ceremonial burning to honour the dead, and the ancient looking Andy Ellis tailors, which had been the place to go to get a zoot suit made in the 1930s. I loved this part of Pitt street for being a pocket of past time, with its archives of secondhand records, the Jazz Garter secondhand clothing store, and the slowly rusting, six-storey high, Hotel Westend sign.

A little further out from the city was the Half A Cow book and record store on Glebe Point Road. It was so small that only a few people could browse inside it at any one time. Half A Cow was, like the other record stores, also a record label, but seemed more like an extended family, united by the unusual symbol of a cow neatly sheared in half. One of the label's early releases, the Smudge song 'Don't Want to be Grant McLennan', was once single of the week in the *NME*. This, like any international validation of something local, only increased its popularity back at home in Sydney. An ode to the impossibility of writing an original pop song, it got my attention for its brevity and nonchalance. It was a fleeting thought set to music, a song written about not writing a song. Half A Cow became most well known for their links to the American slacker pop band the Lemonheads. The Lemonheads' album *It's a Shame About Ray* included songs written by Half A Cow founder Nic Dalton, and Tom Morgan from Smudge. The album included songs about some important Sydney experiences, such as buying drugs in Newtown and falling for Alison Galloway, drummer of Smudge, Waterfront employee, and indie pop dream girl.

Half A Cow records also sold comics and underground literature, novels by Kathy Acker and William S Burroughs, *RE/Search* books about 'Angry Women' and 'Modern Primitives' and other topics it might have been hard to find on the shelves of Dymocks. As well as novels there were plenty of countercultural oddities, like the *Book of the Subgenius*. The deity of the Subgenius was Bob, a pipe-chomping cartoon head with brylcreemed hair, who advocated 'slack' as a form of enlightenment. So convincing were the Subgenius texts to my teenage mind that it was quite some time until I realised they were actually a parody of a religion, rather than a real one.

My other reason to visit Glebe was to shop at the outdoor markets held every Saturday in the grounds of the primary school. Here I'd stock up on bootleg band T-shirts, candles, and recycled paper letter sets printed with unicorns. The markets were a mixture of hippy stalls selling incense, second-hand clothes stalls and people selling tie-dyed singlets and nylon slips. My favourite of all my Glebe market purchases was a skirt made out of purple lace. I called it my 'toilet roll doll skirt' for its similarity to a doll that decorated my grandparents' bathroom, hiding a toilet roll under its lacy skirt.

At the markets and the record stores I gathered up everything I needed: zines, CDs, records, T-shirts, candles, and took them back home to my lair for contemplation. I'd converted my bedroom into a musical shrine, the walls collaged with flyers I'd picked up from record stores and pictures I'd cut out from magazines. Packets of blu-tack went into the construction of this elaborate assemblage, and the white walls I had once painted in a shade called 'Polar Bear' when we moved into the house were now only visible in slivers. My decorated walls, like my rows of cassettes and piles of street press newspapers, were a kind of insulation, protecting me from the outside world.

All Ages Show

As I scanned through the radio dial and read every word of the street press newspapers I was looking for the magical door that would act as an escape hatch from my quiet, suburban existence. I was certain that music would lead me to this door and, the more I listened and read, I would be sure to come upon it.

Reading the *Drum Media* every week I became familiar with the inner-city venues I was too young to go to, pubs with solid landowner names like the Annandale, the Hopetoun and the Lansdowne. More assertive teenagers would either sneak into such venues or write complaint letters into the *Drum Media*, arguing how unfair it was that under 18s couldn't see live music apart from the occasional all ages show. These shows were listed in the Under 18s column in the *Drum Media*, written by Louise Dickinson of *Lemon* fanzine-fame, but I would read through the listings with a feeling of defeat: my mother wouldn't allow me to see bands, and she would have been so horrified that they had names like the Hellmenn and the Hard-Ons that I couldn't even think of how to ask.

While a lot of my time was spent in my room, I'd take any opportunity to go on a car trip. Rarely did driving errands focus on me, usually they were to take my sister to a music lesson or to pick something up from the shops, but I'd come in the car so I could stare out the window. Sometimes we'd drive around the wealthy areas of Turramurra, looking at the big houses. We would try and guess how many times our house would fit inside one of the vast mansions, or just look at them with mute desire. Staring out the car window as house after house slid by I felt like an empty container that could be filled with any kind of identity, as I imagined pulling into the driveway of a different house and stepping into another life altogether.

One day, as my mother drove us along Beecroft Road, I spied two goth boys walking through the park that ran alongside the railway line. Both had thick thatches of dyed black hair and I watched their skinny black figures until the car turned a corner and obscured them from view. I wished fervently I could have jumped out and followed them. For a long time afterwards I thought about the goth boys, wondering who they were and where they had been going. To see them in Beecroft, a suburb equal to Turramurra in terms of excitement, was as surprising to me as if I'd seen two giraffes loping through the park, grazing on the treetops.

A few months later I came across a hand-drawn ad for an all ages show at the Hornsby Police Youth Club in the *Drum Media*. I hadn't heard of any of the bands, nor 'Cosmic Snail Productions' who were putting on the show, but the ad had the right kind of look, drawn with great enthusiasm but minimal artistry. Most importantly, Hornsby was close enough to home for me to concoct a convincing story around it, with so the gig would go undetected by my cautious mother.

In 1993 Hornsby unveiled its newest feature, a monstrosity of a water clock which sloshed and clanged in the centre of the town square. Opinions on this beast were divided, but most people were suspicious of it and the hundreds of thousands of dollars it had cost the council. Almost immediately pranksters began putting detergent into the water, so mounds of foam seethed out of the fountain that lay below the clock. Apart from the addition of the clock, Hornsby was the same familiar cluster of shops and carparks it had always been, and I moved through its different atmospheres with the innate knowledge of a local. The cluttered Granny Mays gift shop with its ever-running beer taps, bottles of jellybeans packaged as sex pills and Magic Eye picture books. The fabric store with the clean smell of new cloth and heavy, glossy pattern books. The subterranean ambience of the lower ground floor in the Northgate Shopping Centre, with the smell of fertiliser from the Kmart gardening department and the birds chattering from the rows of cages in the pet store.

The Hornsby Police Youth Club was a block back from the shopping centre, next to the AMF ten pin bowling alley. I'd been bowling at the AMF a few times, at first hoping that I had finally found a sport I could be competent at, before again sinking into resignation that no such sport existed. I could have fabricated a story about bowling as a cover, but I decided instead to enlist Rachael's help.

Despite the many hours I spent writing in tiny script in my diary about how I was a completely different kind of creature to other people my age, Rachael was a faithful friend. She would wait patiently while I monosyllabically conveyed my miseries over the phone, and was equally as passionate about music. We both loved The Cure, although our tastes differed a bit – she branched off to early Metallica while I went in the direction of shoegaze guitars. On the night of the gig I hadn't concocted a lie so much as omitted certain elements of our planned evening, which I said would be spent at Rachael's house.

Rachael lived in Thornleigh, in a white brick, split level 70s house which backed onto bushland. Whenever I visited we retreated into her room, a small den on the lower level of the house. It felt cosy down there as we listened to music and I browsed her bookshelf of horror and science fiction novels or painted my nails with dark purple polish. Rachael and I would hang out and listen to cassettes, or occasionally do school work. One experiment for a joint science project involved heating ping pong balls in the oven to see how this affected their capacity to bounce. We set up our laboratory in the garage and marked the height of each bounce on the wall with chalk, laughing at the ridiculousness of our scientific investigations.

On the night of the Hornsby Police Youth Club show I'd chosen my outfit carefully. I wore my Meanies T-shirt over a shiny purple dress and my Doc boots, the shoes I imagined connected me with punks the world over. I put on cheap silver jewellery until I jangled. This outfit was the closest I could come to the grunge gypsy look I kept hoping would appear like magic when I looked in the mirror. Rachael was similarly dressed in a band T-shirt, skirt and boots ensemble. Such clothes normally invited condemnation from our peers, and thus I usually dressed with a feeling of defiance. Tonight this feeling had been replaced by hope.

As Rachael's father drove us to Hornsby I was nervous, not knowing what or who we were going to discover. The Hornsby Police Youth Club. Did that mean there would be police? What if we couldn't find the entrance? What if I read the time and date wrong? With my head full of these witterings, we got out of the car and headed towards the PCYC, a brick building with a long pitched roof. The thump of a drum kit came from the basement of the building and we headed towards the sound.

As we went down the stairs towards the basement room, a sharp, angry guitar chord ran out like a sudden rainbow. The room we entered was full of all the local weird kids I'd previously only imagined existed. The kids with mohawks, the kids wearing the band T-shirts, the kids with nose rings and pink hair. In front of the stage, which was a small raised area at one end of the room, a group of them were clustered, slamming together.

After we stood watching at the edge of the room for a while I felt brave and flung myself towards the moshpit. I was jabbed by punks' elbows and shoulders, knocked around like I was a lottery ball. Then my face entered the thick black web of a goth boy's hair and I inhaled the sweet, hairspray-and-cigarettes smell of it. I recognised him from that day in Beecroft. He, and his friend who was also part of the elbows and knees monster of the moshpit, were terrifyingly cool up close. I extricated myself from the crush. The elbows in my side and the goth boy's hair had been my initiation and now I could watch Savage Cabbage from the safety of the wall.

After this night I kept a vigilant eye on the *Drum Media* for more Hornsby Police Youth Club shows. Most of them featured the same bands: Savage Cabbage, Endangered Faeces and Baby Jesus Hitler. Rachael and I went as much for the music as to people-watch. In between bands we would retreat to sit on the fire escape stairs underneath the AMF bowling centre and stare out into the night. The crash of the balls hitting the pins above us punctuated our conversations.

Sometimes more established bands like the Hard-Ons and the Meanies would play in the larger hall upstairs, and once there was an afternoon show held in the carpark behind the Hornsby Police Youth Club for the 'Not So Big Day Out'. A jumping castle had been set up and I watched the unlikely scene of a lone mohawked punk fling himself violently around the inflatable ramparts. Later on I clambered onto the jumping castle myself, but it was much harder to stay upright than I remembered it having been when I was a child. I bounced unsteadily until I fell and grazed my knees against the inflatable vinyl floor. As much as it stung at the time, at school the next week I was proud of the 'jumping castle burn' visible under the hem of my tartan uniform.

Most of the time I felt too painfully shy to make friends at the Hornsby gigs, but one night Rachael and I befriended two guys from Penrith. They were half-brothers, they said, which seemed a strange method of introduction. Penrith to Hornsby was a long way to travel, but at this show two Canadian punk bands of underground notoriety, DOA and NoMeansNo, were on the bill. We sat with the Penrith boys on the steps of the empty apartment building beside the Hornsby Police Youth Club, with the ghostly silence of empty rooms around us, thinking up something to do before the bands started. Too cowardly to attempt vandalising the water clock, we roamed around Hornsby drinking VB longnecks. By the time we returned DOA were on stage. We joined the throng of punks inside. The only song I recognised was 'Fuck You', a much-covered Vancouver punk classic with a simple and catchy two-word refrain. As everyone in the room sung 'fuck you' in unison, I felt the world shifting. Tomorrow, the punks would be in charge.

Music Festival

As much as I pleaded, I was never going to be allowed to go to the first Big Day Out, headlined by Nirvana and the Violent Femmes and held at the Sydney Showground on the day before Australia Day in 1992. Years later I met a guy who had gone to this Big Day Out even though he was only ten years old: his older siblings had taken him with them. Highlights of his year included starting Year Five at school and seeing Nirvana. Even though I was told this story many years later, I boiled with jealousy. I had no older siblings to break ground for me and take me with them to iconic rock festivals.

In a stroke of luck or foresight, Nirvana had been booked to play the festival when they were still a relatively underground band. By early 1992 *Nevermind* was at the peak of its success and the hype around them and the Seattle music scene was huge. The majority of bands that played the first Big Day Out, however, were Australian, and the Beasts of Bourbon, The Celibate Rifles and Died Pretty had prominent positions on the bill. The Big Day Out was a gathering of bands and fans, a manifestation of the forces that had converged to create the universe of 'alternative music'.

While some people in the scene embraced the term 'alternative', others rejected it, writing virulent letters to the street press about keeping grunge out of *Dolly* magazine, bemoaning the popularity of flannelette shirts, and directing 'teeny boppers' back to lycra and Betty Boo where they belonged. The grunge look had become yet another

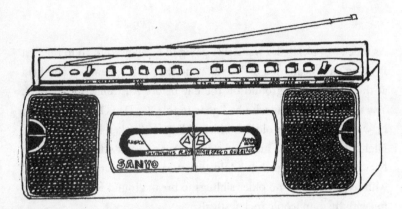

fashion imported from America, although one easy to attain with a visit to a local army disposal store. The music though, at that point in time, seemed angry and alive. For many teenagers there was no going back.

I spent the day of the first Big Day Out listening to Triple J, which had occasional cross-overs to the showgrounds. This experience was unpleasantly reminiscent of Australia Day four years earlier when, instead of joining the millions of people on Sydney Harbour watching the Bicentennial tall ships that had received months of media hype, I watched them on television from my grandparents' living room. The TV was the only source of light in the room, as my grandfather insisted on keeping all the curtains drawn to repel the summer heat. Occasionally I took a photograph of the TV screen, all of which, I discovered upon retrieving the prints from the chemist a week later, came out blurry.

Listening to the radio I felt a deep sense of misery. This didn't lift when I read the reviews that came out in the next week's street press, all of which declared the event to be an unqualified success. Reviewers described the seething, sweaty Horden Pavilion during Nirvana's set, and happy girls walking arm in arm, singing the chorus to 'Kiss Off' by the Violent Femmes as they lurched away from the showgrounds at the end of the night.

The chorus of 'Kiss Off' is a list of grievances, numbered from one to ten: family, loneliness, sorrow, culminating in cries of 'everything! everything!', agonised and joyful at the same time. A live version of the song was played frequently on Triple J and I'd have competitions with myself for how many of the items on the list I could remember. Although the Violent Femmes brimmed with teenage-boy angst I agreed with many of their protests. Sometimes, life didn't feel very fair.

Why, I cursed, couldn't I have been born a few years earlier? I thought of modifications to this wish often, imagining myself in different eras, as a punk wearing garbage bags and safety pins on the King's Road in 1977, a denizen of the Chelsea Hotel in the 1970s, or even just in the audience at the Cure concert at the Bondi Lifesaver in 1980. Begrudgingly I was aware that, in the scheme of things, I was lucky. My life was comfortable and privileged compared to the majority of people in the world. My mother sometimes reminded me of other places and times where we would not have it so easy, such as Nazi-occupied

Europe, for example, or in a world prior to the discovery of penicillin. The thought of a different existence gave me a prickly, weird feeling, like the ghosts of all my possible selves throughout time were watching me as I lay in bed and listened to the radio, sulking about not being able to go to a music festival.

The first Big Day Out I went to was in 1994, headlined by Sound-garden, The Ramones, Björk and The Smashing Pumpkins. Even though none of these bands qualified as my favourites, my anticipation had risen to such a height that the actual day felt unreal. I'd only ever known the showgrounds from Royal Easter Shows: the pavilion where all the regions of New South Wales made pictorial displays out of their agricultural produce; the ring where people congregated to watch trunk-armed men chop trees in the lumberjack contest; the room where the Country Women's Association judged lamingtons with tape measures for the cooking competition. The Big Day Out had an atmosphere not dissimilar. Here people's band T-shirts were on display and we congregated to watch the Ramones play 'Blitzkrieg Bop' as a guy came up out stage dressed as Zippy the Pinhead holding up a sign printed with 'Gabba Gabba Hey'. We could pay $2 to go on an LSD simulation experience that involved sitting in a deck chair and watching a stroboscopic light show through special glasses.

From the looks of the occasional bug-eyed tripper in the crowd, some didn't need to bother with the simulation. As exciting as it was to be up the front for my favourites like the Breeders, for the bands I was less of a fan of I hovered around the dregs of the crowd, where couples had arguments, people with fierce red sunburn drooped, and others deliberated over the program, deciding where to go next. Here I watched scenes like a man carefully arranging crushed VB cans in a ring around a guy who had passed out on the grass. A small crowd had gathered to watch him complete the circle.

The Big Day Out was peaceful compared with the Alternative Nation festival held at Eastern Creek Raceway in 1995. Alternative Nation was an attempt by the promoters and sponsor, Triple M, to cash in on the success of the Big Day Out, even though the station didn't play the majority of the bands on the bill. If the poor ticket sales and uninspiring location weren't enough, it rained on the day and the ground quickly turned to mud. The two main stages were at the bottom of a slope and so the morass was deepest and thickest in front of the stage, an area mostly populated by mud-smeared boys. As well as two main stages there was a number of smaller ones on the top of the hill, where the Australian bands and less famous international bands like Pop Will Eat Itself and Therapy? were relegated. It was less muddy up there, but the stages were small and the sound was relatively weak. In the gaps between songs the sound from the main stage floated over. It was immediately obvious when Bodycount began their set on one of the main stages. Ice-T's voice boomed over, every word a bomb – 'Motherfucker!' 'Bitch!' – as if daring the world to fight back. A few years earlier, Bodycount had caused controversy in America with their song 'Cop Killer'. Many of their songs were about racial discrimination and gang life and were full of the kind of explicit language the black-and-white Parental Advisory stickers were designed for.

Another band that played on the main stage was L7. I first knew of the band from their *Smell the Magic* T-shirt, which had an image of a man's head locked between the thighs of a towering woman. Their songs were tough, like 'Shitlist', a kind of updated, angry version of 'Girl of 100 Lists' by the Go-Gos. The Go-Gos compiled lists of their favourite things and gentleman friends, L7 compiled lists of the many people who pissed them off. In 1992 L7 had played at the Reading festival in the UK, and in response to the abuse and mud being hurled at them from the audience, singer Donita Sparks threw her used tampon into the crowd. Although some of the bands at Alternative Nation were pelted with mud, no one tried it with L7.

At night, fires were lit in drums and people huddled around them, trying to dry off. As Lou Reed's wavering voice sung 'Satellite of Love', I stood around one of these drums with Matt. A few years had passed since our late night driving adventure and over that time we had gradually become closer until we were a couple. He was my first boyfriend and accordingly I was there for him in times of crisis like muddy music festivals. The rain and filth had become all too much and he was considering leaving so I gave him a pep talk, passionately arguing that he would regret it for the rest of his life if he didn't stay to see Nine Inch Nails.

There was a lot of equipment on stage when Nine Inch Nails played and I soon realised that most of it was extra keyboards, put there for Trent Reznor to smash. His own keyboard was mounted on springs so it stretched down towards the ground whenever Trent forcibly pressed the keys. Lights flashed white as he thrashed around, destroying things and singing about angry sex and existentialist angst. Although they had been popular in goth/industrial circles for some time, Nine Inch Nails had recently had an unlikely hit with their song 'Closer'. Despite the explicit lyrics I encountered the song in all sorts of unexpected places, like the Go-Lo in Chatswood Westfield. A song about animalistic sex was the last thing I expected to hear as I stood looking at oil burners in a discount supermarket. It had also been voted as one of the best 'bonking songs' by a Triple J poll, on a list which also included 'Cream' by Prince, and 'Wicked Game' by Chris Isaak. Standing with my boots stuck in the mud at Alternative Nation, listening to people singing along to 'Closer' and flinging mud at each other, the song seemed more like a harbinger of a coming apocalypse than a prelude to love.

While Alternative Nation was an expensive failure for the promoters, the Big Day Out only grew in popularity. By 1996 it had become a summertime institution and a documentary film called

Ritual Habitual was put together, compiling live footage of bands performing and backstage antics. Nick Cave riding a pool pony? Perry Farrell unsticking a joint from his lips and advocating for it to be Halloween every day? The Bad Seeds drummer making a daiquiri? It was both banal and fascinating to see what occurred on the other side of the stage. In some ways it was little different to the kinds of things the punters wandering the showground got up to.

The people I encountered around the showgrounds could be as interesting as the actual performers. Amid the teenagers with spray-in blue hairdye sweating down their faces and the grunge guys in flannelette was the occasional true eccentric. I was particularly curious about a guy dressed in a DIY tiger outfit, a fluffy orange bonnet and shirt daubed with paint. He was dancing around near the trees at the rave tent, underneath the giant dreamcatchers that had been assembled among the branches and a banner reading 'Hearing Protection Must Be Worn in this Area'. Although it was a thriving scene, dance and rave culture was a mystery to me. All I knew about it was that it involved fluoro and the kind of bass beats that shook your very cells. Maybe it also involved tigers.

I was so taken with the tiger that I took a photo of him, and this became my favourite Big Day Out photo of all. Most of my Big Day Out snapshots were of a band playing far away in the distance, a tiny Courtney Love or Nick Cave just visible above a pattern of heads, but

the tiger was much easier to get close to. Years later I rediscovered the tiger photo in a suitcase of old photos. I looked at it closely and realised I knew him. The tiger was my friend Simon, we both worked at the local Salvation Army op-shop. When I showed it to him he didn't seem particularly surprised to see it.

'A lot of people took photos of me that day,' he said, 'even *Dolly* magazine.' That year he had snuck into the Big Day Out, climbing over the showground fence in the early hours of the morning and hiding in the horse stables all night, curled up on a pile of hay, drinking cask wine. Why was he dressed as a tiger? 'The tiger was my alter ego. I often dressed that way.' The 1990s, we agreed, was a time when you could easily maintain such a persona.

I saw people attempting to sneak into the Big Day Out less stealthily, by climbing over the fence as the festival was in full swing. Some were tackled by security guards, others ran as fast as they could into the crowd and disappeared as everyone cheered them on. Some, like the members of the drain-exploring Cave Clan, snuck in through the drains and emerged through grilles inside the showgrounds. Breaking in to the Big Day Out was a badge of honour, with a prestige much greater than other sneaking in tricks, like drawing the stamp onto your wrist to get into a pub gig.

Sneaking into festivals wasn't something I ever tried. After three years my enthusiasm for the Big Day Out burnt out and 1996 was the last one I went to. By the next year I was too goth and sun averse to want to spend all day outside. But still, every year when a new Big Day Out line-up is announced, I scan the long list of performers and feel an echo of my teenage enthusiasm, as I mentally tick off which of the bands I'd most like to see.

Zines

After discovering zines in record stores I developed a fascination with them to rival my love of music. Zine-makers understood that life was anything but neat. This was evident in the chaotic way zines were cut and pasted together as well as the strange or trivial topics that they focused on. My favourite zines were made up of detailed personal stories and obsessions, ones from which I could easily imagine the writer into being, communicating directly to me. By reading zines I could delve into the thoughts of people with similar ideas, or at least with a similar penchant for eccentricity.

One of the first zines I bought from Red Eye Records was *Murder Can be Fun* by Johnny Marr. Not the Johnny Marr from The Smiths, but an American guy who had a fascination with disasters, crimes, eccentrics and weird books. For a special issue of *Murder Can Be Fun* he put together *(Anti-) Sex Tips For Teens*, a zine which compiled ridiculous sex advice for teenagers culled from outdated guides bought from used bookstores. These included books such as *What A Young Man Ought To Know*, published in 1897, which included warnings not to read novels as they weaken the mind, and suggested sleeping on hard beds with minimal coverings no matter the season. On the other end of the spectrum were books from the more permissive 1960s such as *How To Get a Teenage Boy and What To Do With Him When You Get Him*, from which was reprinted a chart of different types of boys. The boys are ranked on a scale from sports superstar to creep, and for each type there is a suggested method of approach. My preferred type from the list was The Shadow, with 'At home' his natural habitat.

Although it was tongue in cheek, this zine contained the most teen advice I'd ever read outside of magazines. It was probably intended for people who'd come out the other side of their teen years, but reading it as a teenager it was surprisingly meaningful, if not actually useful. Current magazines gave me advice that was almost as absurd and useless. *Dolly* and *Girlfriend* magazines had a tone of relentless positivity I found asinine and were full of tips such as using lemon juice to lighten your hair. Women's magazines like *Cosmopolitan* and *Cleo* included sex advice about stripteases and g-spots which was abstract to me: I learnt more from reading the saucy parts in *The Secret Diary of Laura Palmer* or *Flowers in the Attic*.

Almost everything I discovered about being a teenager came from gleanings here and there rather than any direct advice or conversations. I didn't have the kinds of friendships in which we candidly discussed such things. At school I'd sit at the back of class and look over the heads of everyone in front of me, trying to imagine thoughts emanating from their Pantene-scented hair. I struggled to guess what these were.

At school, formal instruction on teen development topics had been minimal, apart from a few science lessons in which the teacher brought in a wicker basket full of different methods of birth control. At my all girls' school it could often seem as if men didn't exist, apart from the occasional teacher and the gardeners. The surfer-guy gardener, with his long, sun-bleached hair, was particularly popular. Once, outside the window of our classroom during an English lesson, he stood in a blue singlet and King Gee shorts, weeding an agapanthus bed. That day it wasn't difficult to imagine the thoughts of my classmates.

Zines became my unofficial guidebooks. In them I found a different way to think about life, one that reflected my own burgeoning identity. I was pleased to feel different from the people around me, even though I was often lonely. There are two types of teenagers: those who strive to fit in and those who don't. As I saw it, fitting in anywhere meant suppressing parts of yourself and, in the world of zines, you didn't have to suppress anything if you didn't want to.

Some zines, like *Rollerderby*, seemed free from any kind of shame or self-censorship.

Issues of Lisa Carver's *Rollerderby* zine were strung together by her manic energy and fearlessness. Sex, violence and death were forever present, even in seemingly innocuous topics like reviews of cats or different interpretations of the indecipherable chorus of 'Blinded by the Light'. As a child Lisa Carver had watched roller derby games on television and the glamour and viciousness of the women on skates had made a lasting impression, inspiring the name of her zine. Lisa wrote about horse-obsessed girls and Mills and Boon cover hunk Fabio, she reviewed her redneck neighbours' arguments and published the

explicit letters she received from readers. The zine also featured Lisa's best friends, the Victorian doll-girl comic artist Dame Darcy and photographer Cindy Dall, who assembled self-portrait photos of herself as the victim of violent crimes.

In disgust at the prevailing slacker ethos of Generation X Lisa developed her own movement, Generation L, the tenets of which included the exclusion of whiners, losers and writing about angst, and advocated being proud and excited and wearing sparkly blue eyeshadow. There was something in *Rollerderby* which, at heart, stressed the importance of being yourself. Embracing the parts of yourself that might find Fabio sexy, or enjoying the brutality within *Little House on the Prairie,* whether those things are considered cool or not. Being self-consciously 'alternative' was merely conforming to another set of rules.

The zines I read in the early 1990s depended on whatever came through music stores. It was relatively easy to find high profile US zines like *Murder Can Be Fun* and *Rollerderby.* Other staples included *Beer Frame,* the zine about odd consumer products like the foot measuring Brannock devices used in shoe stores, and *Thrift Score,* a zine about op-shopping by 'Al Hoff, Girl Reporter'. I liked that she identified herself as a 'girl reporter', it highlighted the 'Harriet the Spy' element of zines, of people devising their own investigations and collecting observations.

Other zines were less about observations and more about empowerment and opposition to mainstream media, especially those that drew inspiration from Riot Grrrl. I first encountered Riot Grrrl reading mentions of it in music magazines. Descriptions varied widely, from it being an empowering DIY movement to a violent, man-hating clique: Riot Grrrls themselves made a point of not communicating with the mainstream media. I didn't find any original Riot Grrrl zines from the US in Sydney but soon elements of it came through, reprints of the manifesto in other zines, Australian Riot Grrrl zines like *Grot Grrrl* and

Thunder Pussy and, of course, the records. Like many misfit teenagers I sat in my room as Kathleen Hanna bawled out 'Rebel Girl' from the stereo and I felt that I was changing something just by listening to it. I'd get up and pace around the room, with a sudden energy I didn't know how to use.

While I had heard of feminism I thought of it as something that had happened before I was born and I knew only cursory images: bra-burning, protests, women in overalls. Most of the influential people around me were women. The only direct male presence in my teenage life was my grandfather, a staunch Yorkshireman in his eighties. I would sit by his side as he repaired clocks and watches at his workbench: I shared his practical nature and love of making and fixing things. The world of my all girls' school often obscured gender inequalities of the wider world, but when I encountered Riot Grrrl I started to notice things. Bands with women members were always asked what it was like to be a woman in a band rather than anything about their music. Men on the street suggested my Doc boots were 'kinky' and I felt too scared to talk back to them. Jokes about blonde women were circulated freely. Girls at school teased me about having a moustache and I viewed my face with newfound revulsion. I began to develop an awareness that things weren't as equal as I had assumed.

It was the DIY aspect of Riot Grrrl that inspired me the most. A lot of Riot Grrrl records were released by Kill Rock Stars. The name said it all;

this music wasn't about worshipping the musicians who made it, it was about the message. Do it yourself, say what you need to say, and don't care if people tell you it's not worthwhile. And, although *Rollerderby* deliberately set itself apart from the Riot Grrrl movement, I took from it a similar message: don't sit back and say 'oh well, whatever, nevermind', get up and do something. DIY was an antidote to impersonal mass media and consumer culture, especially in a world where the term 'alternative' had become a monster, hungry to consume anything marketable from the underground.

One of the prevailing cultural preoccupations of the 1990s was the tug of war between alternative and mainstream, authenticity and 'selling out'. On *The Alternative Music Show,* Wayne DZ would sometimes play 'Make it Safe' by punk poet Patrik Fitzgerald. Recorded in 1977 it described the commodification of punk, which, in the poem, has been eroded to the point where bondage trousers were being sold in Woolworths. Exactly the same process had taken place with alternative music. You could enter the mall in a Sportsgirl shirt, bike shorts and Reeboks, humming 'Achy Breaky Heart' and exit wearing boots and a Sonic Youth T-shirt, a new piercing stinging your nose. While it did offer a different identity for teenagers living in the suburbs, alternative style had quickly became a cliché, another manifestation of the conformity which I had tried to escape from by liking the music in the first place.

The 90s were an era of self-consciousness and obsession with identity and authenticity. Liking things only in an ironic way was a method of personal defence as well as a way to seem knowledgeable about the implications of the kind of trashy, or kitsch things it might be too embarrassing to admit otherwise. Zines were part of an underground world that seemed somewhat free from these preoccupations: or at least in zines it was easier to critique them from the sidelines. Zines existed firmly on the margins, in the same DIY world as community radio and local punk bands playing all ages shows. This was a world of people making things for the love of it, the kinds of things that were too messy, weird, or controversial to be commercialised. *Thunder Pussy* would never be found in Woolworths.

Reading *Rollerderby*, listening to Riot Grrrl bands like Bikini Kill and Huggy Bear, I started to realise that if I wanted things to be different I had to do something about it. I didn't have to look to the US or UK either, there were plenty of local zines, although most were written by people who were older than me and more involved in the music scene. Some of them, such as *The Skills of Defensive Driving,* were available in record shops for free. I nervously slid a copy off the counter in Half A Cow, feeling as if I was shoplifting even though it said FREE eight times on the cover. It was the 'sexy dating issue', and included stories of embarrassing romantic failures. Another free zine was *Ms.45,* a feminist zine 'devoted to anything that pops into my head' with stories about censorship, sex and how to make vinyl records into ashtrays. It was angry and hilarious and reading it felt like overhearing the kind of conversation I might stay on the train past my stop just to listen to more. Zines of personal stories and obsessions were my favourite but I also read plenty of music zines like *Loaded to the Gills, Lemon, DNA, Salty and Delicious, APiTO, TMT, Barcode the World* and *Scrollzine.* I liked the element of chance involved in finding zines: they would be stocked in stores in small numbers, and what was available varied from day to day.

Some of my favourite zines came from Melbourne, such as *Woozy* and *Is That All There Is?* a zine which published answers to questions like 'Please tell me about your worst birthday' and 'Do you know any gossip about your neighbours? Do they know any gossip about you?' I thought about writing to them with the story of how the old fibro house next door had been cut in half and, one night at 2am, the halves had been taken away on the back of a truck, but I felt shy about it, even though the responses in *Is That All There Is?* were mostly handwritten and accompanied by shaky drawings.

After years of reading zines the idea of making my own had been slowly developing. One of the local Sydney zines I read in 1995 was *Penii,* which included everything from band interviews to reviews of Christian propaganda pamphlets and tips for reusing postage stamps. The editor was a guy of similar age to me who lived at home with his parents, and it was perhaps finding out this piece of information that helped me make up my mind.

I called my zine *Psychobabble*, a word I had recently discovered which seemed to fit the way my zine skipped from thought to thought with no particular focus. Most thoughts were of the trivial but persistent sort. Did it hurt one's teeth to use them to break sticky tape? Why did some goth boys think it was a good idea to wear a leather trenchcoat like the guy from *The Crow,* especially in summer? The zine was a balance of my writing and small, ridiculous clippings from a vast array of newspapers and magazines. Rather than use my name for the first few issues I used the pseudonym 'the half master of the universe', inspired by the sample from a Masters of the Universe read-along record at the start of 'Gangrenous' by The Meanies. My sister was the other half, a

division which must have stemmed from a petty sibling arguments about which of us was superior. Another notable music-based sibling argument had resulted in me singing 'Vicious' by Lou Reed to drown out her singing Schubert's 'Who is Sylvia?' as we waited in the car outside the local Coles supermarket. It must have sounded strange to people passing by, a man brought his face up to my window with a look of alarm.

Beyond the purgatory of high school, such small incidents seemed as if they had comprised the majority of my life up until this point. Going to punk shows, shopping for records, reading zines, these were the exciting punctuation marks within my otherwise regular existence. Now in my zine I had somewhere to document the intersection of these two lives. In one *Psychobabble* I recorded a conversation with one of the many elderly citizens of Turramurra which took place in the post office. He'd noticed my Meanies T-shirt and asked 'Are they heavy metal?'

'No,' I said, 'they're punk.'

'Punk,' he replied, 'what might that be?'

As I struggled to think of a meaningful description he said, 'Well, someone's punked,' and moved towards the counter with his bank passbook, leaving me to wonder what on earth he had meant.

I made ten issues of *Psychobabble* in 1996, greatly encouraged by the amount of mail and reviews I received from other zine makers. By the end of the year I had friends who made zines like *Astrogrrrl*, *Circumstantial Evidence*, *The Miraculous Indulgement of the Hairball Goulash*, *Sure*, *Bad Turnip Man*, *Spammy*, *My Life as a Megarich Bombshell*, *Cavity*, *Attractive*, *Nervous Dandruff*, *Dazy*, *Pivetes*, *Fried Trash Tabouli*, *Dazed and Swarming*, *The Burning Times*, *XYZ*, *The Life and Times of Mavis McKenzie*, *A Show of Hands*, *Catpounce*, *Bizarrism* and *Girls with Power Tools*. I spent a lot of time writing letters and walking down to the red post box closest to my house to send them.

It was at the bottom of a hill and I'd usually pass by the black and white cattle dog that liked to lie in the gutter, a mad look in its eye, ready to spring up and start rounding up cars. With each letter posted, a small part of myself went free.

For my tenth issue of *Psychobabble* I decided I would review the 'crassest things in Sydney', a highly subjective tour which included characters like the bronze Il Porcellino hog statue on Macquarie Street, the wax model of the Terminator outside Planet Hollywood on George Street, and the mannequin caveman and dinosaurs on the top of the Kodis Mannequins factory on Cleveland Street, which I referred to as my 'muse and inspiration'.

I ended up visiting the Kodis building often when my friend Tim lived there a few years later, along with most of the members of the goth punk band Cult 45. At night they would sneak into the mannequin factory and explore the piles of arms and legs and torsos waiting to be assembled, and sometimes they'd climb up onto the roof to stand beside the dinosaurs and look out over the streets of Redfern and Chippendale. By now I had moved out of home and, after a few unsuccessful attempts at university, much of my time was devoted to making the last few issues of *Psychobabble* and my new zine *Laughter and the Sound of Teacups*, in which I wrote about everything I did on the 23rd of the month.

I'd sit in the small tacked-on room at the back of the sharehouse I now lived in and type out that month's 23rd story from start to finish.

The room smelt of cigarettes and was cluttered with music equipment; I liked to imagine it had a Berlin, Birthday Party kind of ambience even though it was a terrace house in Camperdown. I wrote stories of going to parties and being attacked by witchy girls clasping Barbie dolls, of having singalong nights to the Cure album *Pornography*, and plenty of Parramatta Road observations. I lived close to Parramatta Road and loved it for its run-down, incongruous assortment of businesses, the combined 'tobacconist and jeanery', the dusty empty shops with years of mail piled up behind the doors and the video store mural of a dinosaur tearing through the wall on the corner of Bridge Road. Further towards the city someone had spray-painted 'Don't move to Newtown' in huge letters on the wall alongside the university. While I was aware that I was probably one of the disdained recent arrivals, I felt like I belonged here. It was the home I had chosen, rather than the one I was born into.

I liked to imagine I had become a Parramatta Road character along with those I wrote about: 'lettuce man' who was often seen with plastic bags full of lettuce leaves, to feed an army of rabbits, I imagined; 'Salvador Dali', a guy with a black moustache waxed into points; and the woman who wore big fake fur coats and walked along Parramatta Road singing arias. Every time I left the house I carried a notebook with me, as anything I noticed could be zine worthy.

By the late 1990s a number of zine anthologies and journals were put together in attempts to document the scene, such as *New Pollution*,

Megazeen and *Milkbar*. *New Pollution* was produced by Octopod, a collective based in Newcastle which also organised the first National Young Writers' Festival in 1998. At first it seemed an unlikely location for a central gathering of underground writers, but as soon as I arrived I understood the appeal. Newcastle was romantic in a post-industrial kind of way, with copious empty buildings and beaches that were perfect for night walks, the waves glowing blue with phosphorescence.

I visited Newcastle for the first time to attend the festival, my bag packed with copies of my zines. As curious as I was about the festival I felt shy about attending; my favourite method of communication was writing zines and letters, and face to face conversations were far more unpredictable. 'Vanessa Psychobabble' was a heightened version of Vanessa Berry, more cynical and sharper tongued, or at least that's how I imagined her. Others had different impressions.

'Before I met you,' Chris from *Dazed and Swarming* told me, 'I thought you'd have blonde hair and wear rainbow tie-dye.' He was surprised to discover the truth, that Vanessa Psychobabble was a sardonic goth.

It could be strange to meet people after reading their zines and matching up their personas with the real person in front of you. I travelled to Newcastle prepared for such situations. I had decided I would only wear red clothes while I was there as a way to channel confidence, but my red outfits were more successful in inspiring comments from cars cruising along Hunter Street. I'd turned up at a discussion about young women in the media, my head still ringing with 'hey peachy arse' and other such insults.

Despite my social nervousness, being in Newcastle for the festival was an adventure. Even staying at the Hunter on Hunter Hotel and being kept awake by the covers band doing an extended version of Depeche Mode's 'I Feel You' didn't annoy me as much as it normally would have, though I fled the dorm room early the next morning when I heard the two people in the bunk below me having sex.

Such experiences gave me plenty of fresh anecdotes to tell, which saved me from the worry of telling people stories they'd already read in my zines. Although the festival had a full program of panels and workshops about things like DIY publishing, getting grants and building webpages, the central activities of the festival were drinking beer in one of Newcastle's decrepit old pubs or hanging out under the fig trees in Civic Park.

The festival event I enjoyed most was the presentation about Young People Against Heavy Metal T-shirts. Matthew Thompson had convinced the mainstream media he was the head of an organisation which campaigned against gruesome heavy metal T-shirts and ran deprogramming retreats for the kids who wore them. We watched a video of a segment that had been broadcast on Derryn Hinch's current affairs show *Hinch* about the movement. This included interviews with members of YPAHMTS, who were played by Thompson's friends in such a convincing way that by the end of the segment – the guy behind the counter in Utopia Records telling one of the YPAHMTS members to get a life – I understood how people could have been fooled.

Although the gap between alternative and mainstream music was debatable, there was a wider and more meaningful division between alternative and mainstream media in the 1990s. Octopod had been set up as a public access media space where people could browse alternative media, in their zine library or on the internet using one of Octopod's computers. At the festival I listened to Rosie Cross from *Geekgirl* zine talk about the possibilities of the internet. The Geekgirl slogan was 'Grrrls Need Modems'. I had a modem but my internet use was limited to emails, posting messages on the zines_aus message board, and looking up song lyrics. To those who made websites, though, the internet was an empowering force for freedom of information.

As exciting as this new form of alternative media was, I stuck to zines. I loved that they existed under the radar of the mainstream press, and thus people published with little fear of censorship or copyright restrictions. Anything that revealed zines to wider exposure could be treated with suspicion by the zine community: articles in newspapers about zines being the new youth phenomenon, academic research into zines or something like the film *Fresh Air*, a movie based around the everyday lives of three people in a sharehouse in Marrickville. The main character of *Fresh Air* made a zine for each day of the week. I grimaced my way through the screening at the Newtown Dendy and wondered what kind of research the filmmakers had done. I'd written uncannily similar things to some of the main character's ruminations, about cheerful butchers, collecting shopping lists, and my fear of walking around with my skirt tucked into my underpants and not noticing it. As we discussed it on the zines_aus message board someone suggested that the possible appropriation was in the spirit of zines, another made the wise point that if I was to give away VHS copies of *Fresh Air* with my next zine, I would no doubt be hearing from their lawyers.

These minor scandals rose up then ebbed away and I kept on making zines regardless. I now lived in Annandale, after I had moved across the creek from Camperdown to an apartment that took up the top floor of a terrace house. It was behind the Annandale Hotel and in the afternoon I could go in and watch the bands doing soundchecks. From the room where I sat to write, I could see Parramatta Road through a gap in the buildings. No matter the time of day or night, the traffic was constant, like a heartbeat.

The first summer I lived in Annandale I embarked on a project to go to every St Vincent de Paul op-shop in Sydney and make the results into a zine. Op-shops were full of cheap treasure, 60s dresses, genie bottles, Tretchikoff prints, weird figurines, ceramic donkeys, piles of boys' and girls' annuals, travel bags from defunct airlines ... All the detritus of the

20th Century seemed available if I looked hard enough, and I quickly filled up our new house with the spoils of my investigations. I used the section of the phone book that listed all the St Vincent de Paul stores as my guide. I travelled by train or bus, having not learnt to drive: another thing that set me apart from my peers as a teenager. By the end of February I had visited 69 stores and made a huge zine about them, *Vinnies*.

Its popularity surprised me. As usual I'd stocked them at Waterfront records, which by the late 90s had the most comprehensive zine section of all Sydney record stores. I left ten copies there, somewhat nervously as usual – I'd never quite got over my reverent fear of record store staff – and thought no more about it until I next went into the store. When I neared the counter, the man who had once told me about seeing Sid Vicious live asked if I was the person who made the op-shop zine.

'People keep coming in and asking for it,' he said. 'All sorts of people. Women who volunteer in op-shops are coming in from the suburbs and asking for it.' He asked me to bring in more as soon as possible.

I liked the idea of op-shop volunteers making excursions to Waterfront records to find my zine. As I stood for hours in Officeworks, page after page of *Vinnies* sliding out from the copier, I wondered what they would make of the snatches of op-shop volunteer conversation I had recorded, my observations of people haggling over the price of control underpants or my disgust at overpriced Globite cases and the smell of the sock basket.

Vinnies was the first zine in which I included my full name. Most people who made zines used either a pseudonym or their first name only, and I was still known as Vanessa Psychobabble in the zine world. I'd made a reference to the fact I had a fruit as a surname but not specified which one, after which I received a few letters addressed to Vanessa Banana.

When people I'd met through zines found out my surname was Berry it surprised me how popular it was. I'd lived with Berry my whole life and it had seemed an utterly normal name until people took such delight in using it, decorating letters with berries – I had a post office box at Strawberry Hills, to compound matters – addressing me by full name only, or ditching the Vanessa part altogether and just calling me Berry.

Once I'd reclaimed my real name, Vanessa Psychobabble, cynical spirit that she was, was tucked away into 90s zine history and I looked forward. Towards the end of 1999 I started work on a new zine, which included the best parts from my journals, lists of interesting strangers I encountered and fictional stories about people whose names I'd collected from the graveyard at St Peter's Anglican Church on the Princes Highway. Between the stories were small black and white family snapshots from the 1940s which I'd found in an album in an op-shop. I didn't know what to call this new zine until I came across a headline cut out from a newspaper which read 'I AM A CAMERA'.

Of all my zines *I am a Camera* has had the longest life; I still put out an issue occasionally. Many times over the years people have asked me about the name. Is it a tribute to Christopher Isherwood? Did I know there was something else with the same name? Is it about cameras? No, I say, it came to me by chance.

The Mudhoney Incident

After we became friends through zines, Chris and I would sit up until late in his room, drinking black coffee and folding up copies of his queer punk zine *Dazed and Swarming* or making cassettes. We'd discovered that you could buy 20c blank cassettes at Reverse Garbage, which we agreed was an incredible bargain. We bought as many of them as we could afford. They were grey and had Royal Blind Society stickers on them, and had been originally used for recordings of magazines read aloud for the visually impaired. We filled them with copies of songs from his record collection, by bands like Propagandhi and Behead the Prophet No Lord Shall Live.

Chris' parents had gone away for a few weeks of the summer, taking his two youngest siblings with them and leaving Chris and his brother, who lived in a caravan in the backyard, to mind the house. They immediately invited their friends over. The house was now populated by a band of scruffy northern suburbs punks and me, the lone goth. Despite this, things were peaceful. A summer lethargy had infected everyone. Someone had dragged the Christmas fir tree out onto the back lawn and left it there on its side – but this was the limit of our misbehaviour.

On one evening as night fell I went into Chris' room to be by myself for a while. A familiar feeling of loneliness had risen up inside me and was being joined by all my darkest worries. So I did what generations of teenagers have done in this situation: I lit candles and put on a record. I flipped past the angry punk records and chose the Mudhoney LP

Every Good Boy Deserves Fudge. Already this seemed like the soundtrack to a part of my life that was far in the past, though it was five years before at the most.

A few songs into the album I tired of staring into the candles and went out to the garden. It was night now and people were passing around a joint and looking at the stars. Out there it was peaceful, with only the soft chug of a train going by in the distance. A mosquito whined past my ear. Then the screen door banged as one of the punks ran out of the house. 'Chris, man, your room's on fire!'

Everyone moved quicker than I thought possible. The smoke alarm screamed as Chris and his brother ran into the house and I stood with my hand over my mouth, knowing it was my fault.

A minute later Chris' brother ran out of the house holding the

record player up above his shoulder, resting on his palm as if he was a waiter delivering a flambé. He threw it on the lawn and someone ran over with the hose and extinguished the flames.

Inside, smoke trailed out of Chris' room and he swatted the hall ceiling with a broom trying to quiet the alarm, which was shrieking at ear-piercing volume. A big swing later and the alarm, and some of the ceiling, had crashed to the floor. We stood looking at it. The smoke alarm had a small black radiation sign on it and a warning that it contained Americium, a detail, had I been feeling less guilty, I would have remarked on. 'This is all my fault,' I said.

Out in the yard the punks were marvelling over the fact that although the record player was destroyed, the Mudhoney record was still perfect, not melted or warped. They were calling it a miracle.

The fire had been mostly confined to the record player and nothing else had been damaged. There was, however, the matter of the hall ceiling, which would almost certainly be noticed by Chris' parents upon their return. The house was brick and Federation era, but surprisingly the ceiling in the hallway was made out of a polystyrene-like substance. A jagged hole revealed the darkness of the roof cavity above.

The next morning we made a journey down to the dumpsters behind the local Coles supermarket. Things were ghostly in West Ryde and the carpark was empty; it felt as if everyone else had fled and we were the only people left. We chose a polystyrene box and back at the house the youngest of the punks, a boy with curly golden hair and a cherubic face, spent a long time with a craft knife, whittling a piece of it into the exact shape of the hole in the ceiling. I sat on the church pew in the hallway, watching him whittle. The pew was an unexpectedly goth home-decorating feature, though Chris' parents were nothing of the sort. They were the serious kind of people who wouldn't appreciate holes in their ceiling.

After a few trips up and down a ladder and refinements with the craft knife, the replacement piece of ceiling was the right shape, and was fitted into place. While it was obviously patched up it was not immediately noticeable and perhaps a story about overenthusiastic pancake cookery or burnt toast would account for the damage. I bought Chris a new record player from an op-shop and we put the Mudhoney incident behind us.

Tear It Up Kitty Cat

The more zines I made the more surprising letters and odd things I received in the post. A heart made of felt with a plastic fly stitched to it. A rubber chocolate stolen from the window display of a Darrell Lea store. A plastic figurine of a shrouded corpse lying on an examination table. I'd put out requests and people would respond: a girl who worked in a Bi-Lo supermarket sent me all the used shopping lists she found while working her shift, as I mentioned in my zine that I collected them.

One letter arrived from a girl called Steph Piecemeal, along with a list of interview questions for her upcoming zine. She told me to answer them without thinking, as if she and I were sitting on a couch watching *Easy Rider* and eating pasta. They were good questions, about how I thought people who read my zine perceived me, and about tastelessly decorated houses. After I sent back my replies we exchanged a few short and friendly letters. She signed hers with 'tear it up kitty cat', a phrase which made me imagine her wearing a leopard-print bikini and drinking a cocktail by a pool.

In 1998 Steph wrote me a longer letter. Among the topics she wrote about she described the horror movies she made when she was a teenager. In *The Aggressive Gardener* she played every role and used the sound of someone biting into a fresh apple to mimic the sound of someone's skull getting crunched. Her vast, funny missive was all the encouragement I needed to write my own digressive letter in return, and from there our letters became longer and longer. She wrote of going to the Arthouse

Hotel and seeing punk and hardcore shows, and nights that ended up in unexpected places. I sent her copies of *Laughter and the Sound of Teacups* and she wrote back that she imagined me like Molly Ringwald's character Andie in *Pretty in Pink*. Reading this, I borrowed it from the video store with the dinosaur mural on the side, and watched the movie again. Andie was like me in some ways, an outsider at school, moving uneasily between her own creative world and the outside world. Unlike Andie, however, I didn't go to my high school prom, and had never regretted this decision for a second.

If I was Andie then I imagined Steph a bit like Iona, her wise and glamorous confidante. Steph did things differently from the other people I wrote to. Her letters were more like zines, but zines made only for me, put together in booklets with pictures from B-grade movies and enigmatic photographs to illustrate them. Steph sent me two movie mix tapes with scenes from her favourite movies. I had been sent cassette mix tapes in the post before, but never VHS. The cases were decorated with blue glitter and hologrammatic fruit stickers, and included scenes from movies as diverse as *Welcome to the Dollhouse, Full Metal Jacket, Ferris Bueller's Day Off, Betty Blue* and *Dumbo*. The second tape began with a scene from *Boogie Nights,* a bungled drug heist to the soundtrack of 'Jessie's Girl' by Rick Springfield at the home of a satin-bathrobe-wearing gangster. Whenever I heard 'Jessie's Girl', in the supermarket, or being belted out by someone doing karaoke in the Egyptian-themed bar at Newtown RSL, I'd think of Steph.

We kept writing letters, but our curiosity about each other had developed in a way that went beyond my usual zine friendships. Even though I still didn't even know what she looked like, apart from the photo of her feet in a pair of scarlet high heels that illustrated one of her letters, it felt inevitable that we would one day meet. Steph also sent me a list of what would happen when we met up. 'Almost immediately you will be struck by how aggravating my phraseologies and mannerisms are.'

But it wasn't like that at all. As awkward as it could be to meet people I'd only known through the post, I was sure we would click, only it was more of an explosion. Steph was like a comet. During the first week we met in person we held a hell-themed dinner party for unsuspecting guests, dressed as metal chicks and went to see an AC/DC tribute band at a scary St Peters pub. We watched *Sid and Nancy* in a room full of yellow balloons and went swimming in op-shop wedding dresses at Bondi beach at dawn after being out all night. The beach was busy with people taking morning walks and going jogging, and they looked at us curiously as we lay side by side in our long white dresses, which were wet and stained with sand. We waited for the snap of the camera shutter to fix us in time, as the waves curled onto the shore behind us.

VHS

The house was dark and I sat close to the TV screen, watching *Twin Peaks*. It was on late and so as not to disturb my mother and sister I had the lights off and the sound down low. While most of *Twin Peaks* was harmlessly odd in the Log Lady, fish-in-the-coffeepot kind of way, the show had a relentlessly ominous feeling about it. Watching it by myself in the quiet house amplified its menace and made the few truly scary scenes almost unbearable.

The worst moment was when Bob came climbing over the floral couch in the Palmer's living room. The pastel, domestic scene – so familiar in its stuffy 80s styling it could have been any house on my street – was ruptured by the leering madman, climbing over the couch and moving swiftly in my direction. At this moment, the dark house around me became full of lurking demons. I was in a panic as I walked down the hallway towards my bedroom and lay in bed sleeplessly for hours, imagining Bob rising up from the foot of my bed or, with every crack of the settling house, about to creep through my bedroom door.

Being a fan of *Twin Peaks* I knew the story of how the character of Bob had been cast. Director David Lynch liked the look of the set dresser crouching down at the foot of Laura Palmer's bed while they were preparing for a shoot, and thus chose him to play Laura's killer. I often pondered this sequence of events, and how it would feel to find your calling acting the role of a demonic murderer. Bob did look wild, with his long grey hair and creepy smile. Even his denim jacket was menacing.

The next morning at school Lynne and I discussed the episode during roll call. Bob was surely Laura's killer, but *who was Bob?* At school I was part of a group of *Twin Peaks* fans who would convene to share our theories over who killed Laura Palmer, or, as the series progressed, what exactly was going on. As the final episode approached Lynne had a sleepover at her house where we stayed up all night watching the episodes she had diligently taped from week to week. Being a *Twin Peaks* fan was like being in a secret society. It was considered too weird by the majority of the girls at school, who preferred shows like *Beverley Hills 90210*, *Baywatch* and *Melrose Place*.

The teenagers in *Twin Peaks* – serious, secretive girls with pale skin, pastel sweaters and woollen skirts – were more my scene than Brenda and Brandon drinking milkshakes in the Peach Pit in *Beverly Hills 90210*. Inspired by *Twin Peaks* I started drinking coffee and referring to it as 'damn fine', like Agent Dale Cooper, who seemed to survive on a diet of coffee, donuts, and slices of cherry pie from the Double R Diner.

As well as appreciating its oddness, I liked the fact that *Twin Peaks* felt more like an entire world than just a TV show. Its many secrets, dark woods and clubhouses harmonised with my suspicion that there were hidden worlds beyond the one I knew. I could inhabit the *Twin Peaks* world easily, my allegiances shifting the more episodes I watched as different characters emerged. I was particularly fond of the agoraphobic

Harold Smith, who spent his time tending to his hothouse orchids before he went crazy, dragged a garden fork down his cheek and committed suicide. Harold was the custodian of Laura Palmer's diary and his decline was triggered when he caught Laura's friend Donna trying to steal it from him.

The diary had a real world manifestation, a book written by David Lynch's daughter. I was so eager to read *The Secret Diary of Laura Palmer* that I shoplifted it – something I had mostly ceased to do after the woman from the South Turramurra newsagent had caught me making off with a copy of *Smash Hits*. This time I was more successful and my theft went undetected. As soon as I had the book I read through it avidly. It documented Laura Palmer's decline from a sweet, good girl to

a high school princess leading a depraved double life in a series of increasingly debauched, then paranoid, diary entries. Feeling a sudden sense of moral responsibility, I told my sister she was too young to read it, although she no doubt sneaked it from my room to find out why.

My other regular late-night viewing was *Rage*. I'd be half falling asleep in front of *Eat Carpet* on SBS, until, at around midnight, it was time to switch over to the ABC. When the flickering screens of blue grey static and distended heads mouthing along to the cries of 'rage' finally appeared I'd sit up, put the VCR onto REC PAUSE mode, and wait for a good song to come on. I'd stay up for hours, watching just one more video until I could stay awake no longer.

On Fridays *Rage* played new releases and on Saturdays guests would program their favourite videos. Some would be chosen often, such as the 'Nick the Stripper' by The Birthday Party, 'Ghost Town' by The Specials, 'The Message' by Grandmaster Flash and the Furious Five, or the live video of Dead Kennedys doing 'Holiday in Cambodia', which I guessed must have been the only Dead Kennedys video *Rage* had. In between the videos the guest programmers would explain their choices. Often this was the most interesting part of *Rage*, watching the Reid brothers from The Jesus and Mary Chain argue whether Morrissey was 'shite' or not, or Frank Black brush his teeth with laundry powder.

My favourite introduction to any song was Henry Rollins explaining why he'd chosen 'November Spawned a Monster' by Morrissey. I loved Morrissey and The Smiths but came to realise he divided opinion like no other pop star. Rollins said that Morrissey 'embodies every horrible trait that a human could possibly possess' before elaborating on what kinds of tortures he would inflict upon Morrissey had he been the director of the video. As it is, the video is of Morrissey cavorting in Death Valley wearing a sheer black shirt, a band aid over one of his nipples and a hearing aid in one ear. Towards the end of the video he sensuously runs his lips along a block of milk chocolate, before writhing in the desert dust.

Sometimes I'd give thought to what videos I'd program on *Rage* if I were given the chance. In the kind of speculative frame of mind that accompanies dreams of winning the lottery or being able to stop time, I'd concoct lists of my top five music videos. Rather than slick and polished videos I preferred clunky and DIY, like the video for 'Charlotte Sometimes' by The Cure. Fiona and I laughed about its stagey sense of disquiet, the band standing like black-clad ghosts in an abandoned school while a schoolgirl with long crimped hair discovers her past self in the mirror. My favourite video was for 'Punk Rock Girl' by The Dead Milkmen, a literal rendering of the events of the song, in which the protagonist and his punk rock girl run amok on the streets of Phila-delphia. They meet at Zipperhead, the punk clothing store, are refused tea in the pizza shop and ask for Mojo Nixon in the record shop (only to be told he doesn't work there). My favourite scene in the video was of the punk rock girl's boots as she jumps up and down on a table in the pizza shop, protesting the lack of tea. I might not have been as cool as the punk rock girl, but I at least had the same boots.

When I couldn't stay up I'd tape *Rage* and watch it the next day. The bluish tinge of the guest programmer segments and the *Rage* theme music made it feel like 3am no matter how sunny and bright it was outside.

Many of the songs I watched in fast forward, despite warnings that this would stretch the tape. VCRs came with a lot of rules and tips for optimisation. LP mode, which doubled a tape's recording time, apparently produced a lower quality picture, but to me it was a kind of magic that enabled me to record far more on my limited number of tapes.

I'd try to fit as much as possible on one video, which could include segments of *Rage* or other music shows like *The Noise*, movies like *Working Girl*, *St Elmo's Fire* and *The Breakfast Club*, episodes of *The Late Show*, *The Young Ones* or *Red Dwarf* and the kinds of telemovies which played outside of prime time. My sister and I particularly enjoyed one we had taped called *Shattered Innocence: Diary of a Porn Queen*, a late 80s film about the career of a porn actress. We watched the film so many times we could quote whole sections of the dialogue. Our favourite was the moment when the not-yet porn queen cries 'you said *semi* nude!' when asked to take off her cowboy costume at her first photo shoot.

We spent a lot of time watching the same movies over and over. Another movie we'd quote from a lot was *Sid and Nancy*, a movie dramatisation of the life of Sid Vicious and Nancy Spungen. Our favourite was the one line spoken by Courtney Love at the end of the film, when Nancy's body is being carried out of the Chelsea Hotel. 'She was really nice!' wailed Courtney, who played the role of one of Nancy's friends. Fiona and I would howl this at random moments, attempting to perfectly mimic the intensity of Courtney's cry.

Other movies we had on tape and would watch over and over were 80s comedies like *Parenthood* or *A Fish Called Wanda,* and Australian mini-series like *The Leaving of Liverpool, Brides of Christ* and *Bangkok Hilton*, a drama starring Nicole Kidman about a woman imprisoned in a Bangkok jail for drug smuggling. Fiona and my tastes only differed in one genre: she didn't share my enthusiasm for horror movies.

I read a lot of horror novels in my early teens – sitting in the backyard with Clive Barker's *Books of Blood* or Stephen King's *Pet Sematary* while eating snack-sized packets of potato chips – and I also watched plenty of horror movies. Fiona was sensitive to horror, even the rice-as-maggots scene in *The Lost Boys* made her look away in disgust. A late night viewing of *Carrie*, and the scene where the bucket of pig's blood is tipped over Carrie as she is crowned prom queen, gave her nightmares for months. I wasn't impervious to fear either. The first time I saw *Nightmare on Elm Street*, watching it on VHS with my school friends, I lay awake the whole night afterwards thinking about Freddy's knife-hands scraping along the pipes.

The *Nightmare on Elm Street* movies made a particular impression among my friends: finding out I hadn't seen it, Rachael described to me in avid detail the scene in the third film where Freddy uses a boy's veins as puppet strings. Lynne and I went to the cinema to see *Freddy's Dead: The Final Nightmare,* the last of the Elm Street films, in 1991. By now the series had become stupidly kitsch. The film was mostly a platform for

Freddy's one-liners and references to pop culture, such as when he traps a boy in a video game and mid-way through unleashes what he calls the 'power glove'. Of course the power glove is his signature knives rather than the Nintendo gaming accessory.

Lynne and I often went to the cinema together on our music and bookstore trips to the city. Our usual destination was the Hoyts on George Street, where we'd see blockbuster movies like *Terminator 2: Judgement Day* or more arthouse films like *My Own Private Idaho*. I was particularly eager to see *My Own Private Idaho*, the Gus van Sant film about two hustlers played by Keanu Reeves and River Phoenix. Lynne's older brother had already seen the film and hated it so much that he had left mid-way through. This made me determined to like it: Lynne's brother had a particular hatred of me and referred to me as the 'goth transvestite'. Whether it was because he thought I looked masculine or that my makeup was garish I don't know. As with most insults that centred on my weirdness, I took it as a compliment.

Regardless of my desire for revenge I enjoyed *My Own Private Idaho*: you could either watch it for the teen heartthrobs or as a meaningful cultural critique. I watched the film again on video ten years later and wrote about it in one of my last *Laughter and the Sound of Teacups* zines. I discovered then that it was one of those films that almost everyone I knew had a story to tell about it. My friend Tim told me a story of going to see it at the cinema in 1991. During the campfire scene in

which River Phoenix's character announces to Keanu 'I really want to kiss you man', a girl sitting behind Tim in the cinema had sighed, full of yearning 'So do I.'

Along with record stores, George Street Hoyts was one of the first places where I felt connected to a culture outside of the safe suburban world I had grown up in. In addition to the cinemas, Hoyts was a vault of arcade games and little shops selling things like death metal CDs and silver jewellery. At the jewellery store at the entrance to the cinema I bought the linked silver rings known as Russian wedding rings, ankh pendants, and the studded black leather wristband that was one of my most prized possessions. The only other place I knew of that sold punk jewellery was Let It Rock, a shop in Centrepoint Arcade, which also sold pots of Manic Panic hair dye. I'd look at the pots of Manic Panic and imagine my hair purple, or red, or blue, although such a transformation was too risky, as I went to a conservative school where any kind of hair-dye was forbidden. Breaking the rules was usually more trouble than it was worth.

My greatest moment of hair rebellion was to put my hair into dozens of tiny plaits, a style for which I was immediately sent to the year coordinator's office and told I had to remove them. I was often in trouble over my hair, although usually because I liked to wear it hanging over my face as a kind of shield from the outside world. I had amassed quite a collection of the bobby pins which they gave me every time. The plaits might have pulled the hair back from my face, but they too were unacceptable to the pedantic dress code of my high school.

My plaited hairstyle was inspired by Casey Niccoli, a woman who was the envy of 90s alterna-girls, with her long purple braids and pale, beautiful face. She was the lover and creative muse of Perry Farrell from Jane's Addiction. She'd directed the video for their song 'Been Caught Stealing', which stars a cast of weirdos on a supermarket stealing spree:

a cartwheeling granny, a pole dancing girl lasciviously squeezing oranges and a man dressed as a pregnant woman stashing things in his foam bump. Another Jane's Addiction video, 'Classic Girl', was of Perry and Casey's voodoo wedding in Mexico and when it played on *Rage* I'd stare deeply into it, trying to notice every detail I could. Everything, from the egg rolled over Casey's forehead at the start of the video to purify her, to their eventual plunge into the swampy lake water in trails of ceremonial smoke, I stored in my repository of details for a fantasy life. In this life I had the same lunar beauty as Casey, my goth boyfriend and I would take part in rituals and live in a house cluttered with spooky, beautiful objects: oil bead lamps, weird sculptures, Mexican tin hearts.

The 'Classic Girl' filmclip was an excerpt from Perry and Casey's film *Gift*, another VHS tape I watched over and over again. *Gift*'s premise is that one night, while Perry is out recording with Jane's Addiction, Casey overdoses on heroin. When he returns later that night, a bunch of daisies picked from a front garden sagging in his lace-gloved hand, he discovers her dead. 'No God, Casey no, oh God no,' he moans. Always at this point in the film, no matter how many times I'd watch it, I felt a shiver of awareness that they were acting out a fantasy. While at the end of the film a screen flashes up purporting the persons and event shown in the film to be fictitious, it is more than obvious that the couple are playing themselves.

All this was fascinating to me, from the opening scene of Perry and Casey driving their white Cadillac through the back streets of Los Angeles, looking to score, to the shrine Perry makes around Casey's body with flowers and lace, Catholic icons and plastic dolls. The film had a lot of graphic drug use and a notorious scene in which Perry, after he has found Casey dead, drags her to the shower and makes love to her. The R rating on the video cover, for 'drug use and adult themes', didn't seem to cover half of it.

Although R-rated films were meant to be restricted to those over 18,

it wasn't hard to borrow them from the local video store. The store had a dimly lit, cluttered atmosphere and I'd await the release of new films onto VHS with great anticipation. My hope was to one day get my hands on one of the cardboard cut outs that advertised new releases – a life-size Keanu from *Bill and Ted's Bogus Journey*, or even a Wayne and Garth from *Wayne's World* – but someone always managed to get in first and write their name and phone number on the back, thus claiming them.

I'd borrow anything that had even the vaguest connection to music, movies like *Repo Man*, which had a soundtrack that included Iggy Pop and Black Flag; *Christiane F* which had the extra excitement of being about a teenage junkie in West Berlin, as well as featuring David Bowie; or *Romper Stomper*, a film about violent, racist skinheads in Melbourne, starring Russell Crowe as the psychotic gang leader Hando. If any music documentaries were played on TV I was sure to record them, whether it be a show about The Lemonheads, with 13 year old Ben Lee in his bedroom singing his ode to Evan Dando 'I Wish I Was Him', or one about Einstürzende Neubauten, with footage of a performance with angle grinders and other machinery on the autobahn, their breath white in the winter cold.

As the 1990s progressed, films that attempted to document the time appeared such as *Singles*, a romantic comedy story set in Seattle during the grunge era, or *Reality Bites*, in which the characters endlessly discuss their problems and relationships. The movie poster for *Reality*

Bites showed the three characters involved in the love triangle that is the main theme in the film standing in front of a wall with keywords on it – love, trust, credit cards, decaf – including, self consciously, 'movie poster'. Most of the film was awkward and self conscious, with occasional moments of relief like the wacky scene in which they dance to 'My Sharona' in the convenience store.

Convenience stores figured large in American films. Strange things were afoot at the Circle K in *Bill and Ted's Excellent Adventure*; in *Heathers,* JD explains to Veronica that the only constant in his life is the Snappy Snack Shack, as he buys her a cherry slushie. There was even a whole film about convenience stores, *Clerks*, shot in lo-fi black and white as if it was CCTV footage. Nothing exciting ever happened at my local convenience store, the Turramurra Quix, but I'd hang around there anyway, drinking Slurpees out the front as I watched the huge rotating brushes of the car wash descend upon the vehicles inside, hoping someone interesting might appear. If I couldn't relate to the characters in Generation X films, I could at least try to relate to their locations.

The film that came closest to how I felt about life and that fast became my favourite was an Australian film from 1996, *Love Serenade*. It was the story of two sisters, Dimity and Vicki Ann, who live in a small town called Sunray. Their new neighbour is a recent arrival to the town, radio DJ Ken Sherry, a jowly, world-weary man who has a deep, love-song-dedications kind of voice. On the local radio station he plays AM radio classics interspersed with his meditations on life. Both sisters fall in love with him and are seduced one after the other on his brown leather couch, underneath his feature wall decoration, a large stuffed marlin.

Of the films about radio, something like *Pump Up the Volume* should have been more relatable for me – a girl listening to a mysterious late night radio show and writing letters to the host – but it wasn't the radio element of *Love Serenade* I liked so much as the weirdness of the two sisters and their isolated country town life. Sunray was a town of silos, deserted train tracks and empty picnic grounds. In that environment anything new, even the leathery Ken Sherry, could be seen as a kind of salvation from everyday life. I'd read an interview with the film's writer and director Shirley Barrett in which she said that one of her inspirations for writing the film was reading the agony aunt letters in women's magazines. She was particularly inspired by one letter where a woman described a recurring dream in which a marshmallow inside her head kept getting bigger and bigger. The movie's central theme was something I felt keenly: life's essential, everyday strangeness.

I considered *Love Serenade* my movie, in that I usually watched it by myself and didn't want to share it with others in case they didn't like it. Whatever I got from it I felt was almost impossible to explain. It was the same with my favourite band, Throwing Muses. When I listened to their albums I felt shivery and their surreal, sharp songs made me feel a surge of energy and understanding. Yet other people listened to them, heard only guitar rock, and felt no magic.

Some movies I only ever watched with other people. *Dogs in Space* for instance, which I first watched in the 90s, was made in the 80s and was about the Melbourne punk scene in the late 70s. The first time I saw it was at Vic's place, a house with asparagus plants growing tall in the garden and the door always open. Matt had become friends with Vic after interviewing him on the radio, and we visited his house increasingly often. Vic never seemed to wear shoes and spent a lot of time writing songs, my favourite of which was a waltz with lyrics that went in reverse alphabetical order from Z to A, telling the story of a character called Romantic Roosevelt.

The house was full of music equipment and upstairs was a loft room accessed by a perilously skinny ladder. Up there was where Vic retreated to sleep, a skeleton draped in a purple robe watching him from the corner of his room. In some ways Vic's household was not dissimilar to the one in *Dogs in Space*. It was its own little universe, host to a revolving cast of characters, any of whom could be up at any time of day or night, playing music or sitting around drinking whiskey.

On New Year's Eve we went round to Vic's house. The video of *Dogs in Space* was playing on a television so flickering that it was hard to see what was happening on the screen, but most of us had seen it so many times that listening to it was good enough. Lines from the movie would break into our conversation, the man extolling the virtues of his chainsaw, a neighbour complaining about their 4am revelries, scraps of songs like 'Pumping Ugly Muscle' by the Primitive Calculators and 'Mr Clarinet' by The Birthday Party, raucous party scenes full of insults, and news updates about the Skylab satellite, which is due to crash to Earth during the film's climactic party.

At the end of the movie, as Anna's death from a heroin overdose is soundtracked by Iggy Pop's 'The Endless Sea', the clock turned to midnight. We left the tape running and walked barefoot out to the street. The harbour fireworks bloomed from behind the silhouettes of trees and we stood watching them. Vic's neighbour – the woman who was worried her ornamental plate collection would fall off the wall when his band rehearsed – wished us happy new year and all the best for 1997.

Death Rock

As a child I exhibited all the warning signs. I was bookish, shy, and given to concocting elaborate tales about orphans and unfortunate children. Drawn to morbid details, I would reread the passage in Roald Dahl's *The Witches* where the boy feels himself turning into a mouse with a thrilling feeling of terror. Imagine being powerful enough to cast such a spell, I thought, and hoped that as I grew up I'd develop witchlike powers.

The development of my powers advanced due to a chance discovery at a Hills Grammar school fête when I was seven. The afternoon was already notable as I'd had my first experience of claustrophobia inside a giant inflatable caterpillar. The other children inside the caterpillar had giggled and shrieked their way through the series of inflatable rooms but I had felt as if I was in a large, vinyl coffin. The caterpillar would have been my one abiding memory of the day if I had not picked out two books from the box of free things at the white elephant stall. A book about witchcraft and a book about fortune telling. These books, with chapters about hexes and the casting of lots, illustrated by black and white photos of gypsy women in trances, became my obsession. I'd sneak the candles that were stored in the pantry in case of blackouts into my room, along with a box of matches from my father's smoking corner. With this equipment I would try to tell my fortune by looking at the reflection of a candle flame in a bowl of water. While the reflections remained stubbornly obscure, the water could well have shown a Bauhaus T-shirt and bottle of black nailpolish.

Many goths can trace their goth identity back to childhood feelings of difference. I certainly felt this way. School was an exercise in masking my personal obsessions, trying to get out of sports classes and being all too aware of my weirdness. Despite the pain of this awareness I never wished to be like everyone else. In primary school I spent most lunch times with another outcast girl, staring at the large, smooth pebbles in the garden beside the art room. Some of these rocks, we decided, were poisonous and would kill you instantly if you touched them. Having convinced ourselves of this we would close our eyes and reach out for the rocks in a kind of Russian roulette.

As a teenager, music was my refuge from the normal side of life I had always felt so little in common with. Goth was something I knew about only vaguely, until a 1992 issue of *Drum Media* with Frente on the cover promised, in the bottom right corner, 'the inside goss on goths'. I loved The Cure but my knowledge of goths did not stretch far beyond their black thatch hairdos, so I was eager to find out more. The article was based around a visit to the Sydney goth club Sanctuary, although it started off with the confusing assertion that although the people at Sanctuary looked gothic and liked goth music, they were definitely not goths. It took me years to figure out that to be truly goth is to deny that you are one, especially to the outside world.

By the time I was reading 'the inside goss on goths' the subculture had been firmly established for at least ten years. The archetypal goth club was the Batcave in London, which had been one of the establishing forces in the burgeoning goth scene there in the early 80s. The Batcave pinup boy was Johnny Slut of the band Specimen, with his towering black deathhawk hair, spiderweb makeup and tight, tattered black clothing. Sanctuary was Sydney's version of the Batcave, and the *Drum Media* article was accompanied by photos of guys in black eyeliner and girls wearing long black dresses and layers of lace and silver jewellery.

Goth appealed to the morbid side of my nature and my love of dressing up, but I was also drawn to it because of its mysteriousness. Even though bands like Nirvana and Alice in Chains were labelled 'alternative' they sold as many albums as Meat Loaf and Bette Midler. As much as I tried to tell myself alternative music was a secret, there came a day when I could no longer ignore the fact it was nothing of the sort.

In my crusade to avoid as much of school sport as possible, I had again got out of swimming by telling the teacher, a hulking, angry woman who smelt of mint Extra chewing gum and cigarettes, that I had my period. 'Some of you,' she growled, looking at the row of pool-averse girls cowering on the concrete steps, 'seem to be constantly menstruating.' It was still preferable to face her wrath than face the changing rooms, where the alpha girls took delight in pointing out the bodily imperfections of the weak.

As I sat on the concrete steps, a group of these girls floated in the shallow end, singing. It took me a moment to recognise the song, but when I did I felt cold with horror. They were singing The Boys Next Door's song 'Shivers', which had been recently covered by commercial hard rock band The Screaming Jets and was in the singles chart. 'I loooove that song!' one of the girls cried out, and joined in with the chorus.

Having something you love stolen by people you hate is a dreadful thing. I loved The Boys Next Door's slow, creaky version of the song, with vocals that always threatened to waver off key. The Screaming Jets did a tidy rock version that bled the song of its uneasiness and made it suitable for tanned, blonde schoolgirls to sing in pools.

Goth seemed a safe place to hide. The popular girls would never float around in the pool singing 'Last Exit for the Lost' by Fields of the Nephilim. Fields songs sounded like an impending storm, with imperious, evil lyrics growled over the top of the music. They wore cowboy boots, long coats and wide-brimmed hats over which they tipped bags of flour, to simulate dust.

As I was far too young to go to Sanctuary, my knowledge of goth came from listening to the community radio show *Sacrament*, one of the pivotal forces in the Sydney goth scene. I made mix tapes of my favourite songs, the yelping panic of 'Romeo's Distress' by Christian Death, the soft, drowning 'Medusa' by Clan of Xymox. Goth songs were night songs, their textures reminded me of clothes, some velvety, some scratchy and lacy; I listened to goth more and more and left other genres behind.

I still liked punk, but its spikiness overwhelmed me. Goth's dark energy was a comfort as I had unexpectedly become very sick. Tired all the time, I was often too weak to go to school and, although this situation would have delighted me a few months earlier, I was afraid of constantly feeling too tired to do simple things. Many tests and visits to specialists later I was eventually diagnosed with Chronic Fatigue Syndrome by a reticent immunologist. After delivering the diagnosis, he stared at me and said 'Well, what are you going to do about it?' I struggled to answer. Ashamed of having an illness that many believed not to exist, a deep, sad well took shape inside me.

While the *Drum Media* article about how goths are normal, cheerful people on the inside seemed somewhat disingenuous, goth gave shape to my feelings of loneliness and sadness, and transformed them into a source of strength. It made it easier to be unhappy if I could mythologise the experience. Goth suited my new, often bedridden lifestyle. Of all music-based subcultures it was the only one in which reading played an important role, and reading was about the only activity I could do without struggle.

My book collection was a mixture of horror novels, books I'd borrowed from my high school library and never returned, and books linked to Robert Smith and The Cure. The Cure had obvious literary influences, Camus, Baudelaire, Dylan Thomas. When I bought a copy of *The Outsider* from Chatswood Book and Record Exchange I was acting

ALBERT CAMUS
The Outsider

out a classic scene. Teenager, in black, approaches bookstore counter, Camus in hand. There was a song on the Cure album *The Top* called 'Banana-fishbones', and so I duly bought a secondhand copy of J.D. Salinger's *9 Stories* to add to the copy of *The Catcher in the Rye* I had permanently borrowed from the school library. I had a crush on Holden Caulfield and when I read *The Catcher in the Rye* I imagined myself beamed into the story, a saviour girl who could commiserate with him about the dominance of phonies in the world. In books and films it was the odd characters who were always my favourites, like the morbid teenage aristocrat Harold from *Harold and Maude,* or Lydia, the ghost-befriending goth girl in *Beetlejuice.*

Over time I collected all the requisite goth items. A long black velvet skirt from Glebe Markets. Op-shop gloves and black lace nightgowns. A round silver pendant inscribed with cryptic markings, sold to me as a 'pendant of knowledge'. Black plastic bracelets, the kind known as 'fuck bands', the schoolyard legend being that if someone broke one, then you had to have sex with them, although I knew no one who took this seriously. I wore inches of these bracelets and, like the knowledge pendant, they became my protective talismans.

Nick Cave was famously quoted as saying that, after the nuclear bomb hit, all that would be left would be goths and cockroaches. I felt almost that tough wearing black clothes, silver jewellery and boots, Sisters of Mercy songs going around in my head. There was something bombastic about The Sisters of Mercy which made me think of sermons. This impression might have come from the video for 'This Corrosion' which was played on *Rage* now and then, and featured the band in a dystopian London of destroyed buildings and spot fires. Andrew Eldrich made grandiose gestures among the ruins as rain poured down over his mirror shades and waxy white chest. All Sisters of Mercy videos had a propensity towards grand statements, although sometimes confusing ones: the video for 'Dominion' was filmed in the rock palaces of Petra and featured Eldrich in a white suit hiding behind columns as the band's bass player, über-goth Patricia Morrison, rode through the desert on a white horse accompanied by men on camels. While to outsiders goth seemed straightforward – black clothes and hair and white makeup – there were plenty of confusing nuances.

I needed to feel tough to appear in public as a goth. Even in quiet Turramurra there was something about the sight of a girl wearing all black that incited the many teenage motorists who had recently attained their P-plates. A simple walk from my house to the post box would be enough to attract a 'Morticia!' from a boy driving his parents' station wagon along Kissing Point Road, or screams of 'goth!' from a hatchback full of girls. These taunts I took as compliments.

As with my earlier musical obsessions, band T-shirts continued to be an important manifestation of my identity. My Alien Sex Fiend shirt met all my goth style requirements: dark, messy, and obscure. The thin fabric soon developed holes and this pleased me, as I could wear it with ripped stockings and layers of black lace petticoats and feel appropriately post-apocalyptic. When I wore it I felt I was a real goth. For although I wore only black, listened to goth music and read everything I could about goths and goth interests, my feelings of having made it could be easily destroyed. All it took was encountering goth girls in their 20s, in beautiful gowns, with excellent control over their liquid eyeliner. They would float past me majestically, while I felt like a little rat. An Alien Sex Fiend rat.

Alien Sex Fiend were a trashy, electro goth band from the Batcave scene in London whose core members were a couple known as Mr and Mrs Fiend. My favourite song of theirs was 'Now I'm Feeling Zombiefied', a song that culminated in screaming out the title over and over, as many of their songs did. I was sure I knew more about being zombiefied than the majestic older goth girls, even if they could do their makeup as perfectly as Siouxsie Sioux. Most of my time was spent either fatigued in bed or at school, struggling to stay awake during epic assemblies bracketed by hymns.

On the days I was well enough to go to school my favourite part of the day was lunchtime, when I would retreat into the art rooms to work on my paintings. Studying art meant I had to produce a major work for assessment, and I was creating a triptych of richly coloured dreamscapes, inspired by the little-known female surrealist painter Kay Sage. The paintings had a long, embarrassingly indulgent title, culled from one of Sage's poems: 'I have built a tower on despair, you hear nothing in it, there is nothing to see, there is no answer when, black on black, I scream, I scream, in my ivory tower'.

There was a paint-splattered cassette player in the art room, and I'd bring in tapes of *Sacrament* to listen to while I painted. I'd almost forget I was at school until some detail brought me back to the present, like someone at the window bellowing 'that girl's *still* in there' to her friends. Mostly I was left in peace to listen to Bauhaus songs and paint spectral hands twined with ivy.

Bauhaus were one of the most enduring goth bands and had I been asked to choose one song to explain what goth was all about (I fantasised about people asking me such questions), it would probably be their song 'Bela Lugosi's Dead'. It is sparse and drawn-out, with horrible creaks and tocks that evoke a cavernous, freezing, stone castle and an elderly vampire in a high collared coat creeping up the stairs. On the cover of the single of 'Bela Lugosi's Dead' is a ghoulish winged silhouette, patchily printed like a decaying old photograph. I had the same image on a T-shirt. Sometimes I wore it under my school uniform in a private gesture of rebellion.

The song's bleak atmosphere neatly encapsulates the kinds of things that goths fantasise about: bats, tombs, silent-film-era horror. Suburban Sydney with its endless sunny days seemed far away from all that, but one of the things that appealed to me about goth was that it was a subculture in which it was acceptable to inhabit an imagined world, separate from the real one. It was acceptable and normal to spend the majority of one's time inside, reading, with the occasional slice of toast to keep you alive. It was also the only subculture where being pale, weak and sickly was beneficial, even desirable. And although the Sydney suburbs had little in the way of cathedrals and castles, there were vacant lots and empty houses, graveyards and gloomy pockets of bushland.

Despite my eligibility, I was a lonely kind of goth, and my connection to the scene was mostly listening to *Sacrament* and reading *Ex Cathedra* or *Dark Angel* fanzines in my room. Occasionally

I would have encounters with real, adult goths, the kind who had been Sanctuary regulars and lived in houses with rooms draped in black velvet, decorated with skulls and crucifixes. For this I had Matt to thank, as he was friends with plenty of goths through his radio show, and I'd sometimes go with him when he went to visit them. The goth household he visited most often had no black velvet but it did have a line of dolls on tiny crucifixes in the front garden and an arm dangling from the manhole in the hallway ceiling.

I'd sit invisibly in the corner of the room, saying nothing but taking in every detail. It was funny to see goths doing normal things like eating dinner, or glimpse their real names on electricity bills affixed to the fridge. Goth girls named Letitia or Lucretia, goth boys named Morpheus or Zillah, all of them hid a Jane or a Daniel inside. Each of them had probably come from a suburban life like mine, but now they lived in a world of their own choosing.

As I sat in the corner I thought about all this while I patted the voiceless member of the goth household, the black dog. The dog and I were silent presences in the room as the goths talked about their band and told stories like the time they found a signed Damned poster on the street during a council clean up – surely the luckiest night of their lives.

Another time I went with Matt to meet up with a group of goths and see *The Nightmare Before Christmas*. We waited in the lobby of the Greater Union cinema on Pitt Street with Leigh, the presenter of

Sacrament, for the others to arrive. I spied their skinny black spider legs and explosions of blue-black hair from a distance.

When they reached us Matt said hello to one of the guys he knew, who stared at him vacantly for a few moments before saying, 'Matt ... sorry man, I'm tripping.' As the film progressed I snuck looks over to the tripping goths, their eyes huge and glassy.

Goths, I discovered, were a diverse group. The girls ranged from ice queens in corsets with huge mantles of black hair, to horror kitsch girls with bats sewn onto their dresses, to sweet, friendly girls who liked the Muppets. The boys were a similarly mixed bunch, from minimalists in black jeans and T-shirts to vampire obsessives who wore capes lined with satin and accessorised with claw-handled walking canes.

While I never felt much affinity for vampires myself, they were an integral part of goth culture. The film version of Anne Rice's novel *Interview with a Vampire* was released in 1994, making over Tom Cruise and Brad Pitt into Lestat and Louis. I dutifully went to see it but, as hard as I tried, I couldn't see Tom Cruise as a convincing vampire. My copy of the novel *Lost Souls* by Poppy Z Brite, however, with its rock star vampires and wayward teenagers with names like Nothing and Ghost, fascinated me. The vampires in *Lost Souls* drive around in a black van listening to Bauhaus, their existence a haze of drugs, sex and blood. I was equally as intrigued by the author bio in the front of the book, listing Brite's previous jobs: 'gourmet candymaker, mouse caretaker, artists' model and exotic dancer' and the fact that 'Poppy Z Brite lives in the French Quarter of New Orleans with two cats and two boyfriends'.

Her reality was ultimately more interesting to me than the fiction; I was curious about how goths lived. Some had day jobs, anything from call centre phone operators to security guards, computer programmers to nannys. I was attracted to goth as an escape from normal, everyday life, but it seemed impossible to be free from conventional reality entirely.

In early 1995 a magazine article about goths, entitled 'Hot Gothic', appeared in *GQ* magazine, inspired by the film release of *Interview with a Vampire*. The article provided an introduction to the scene, describing a house with coffins in the living room and noting that, on the way to the magazine's photo shoot, the goths moved their hands out of the sun which shone through the car window. Underneath a photo of these goths having a mausoleum picnic was a quote from an American goth zine: 'If you have scars on your wrists, by all means display them proudly. Abscesses, however, should always be coyly veiled in filmy black fabric.'

At the same time I was reading this advice so was Natasha, living hundreds of kilometres away on her family's farm near Wagga Wagga. A few years later we became goth accomplices after we met through zines. She, like me, had grown up making mix tapes from the radio and reading music magazines obsessively. We'd quote lines from 'Hot Gothic' to each other sometimes, the line about the abscesses and one about goths always getting a seat to themselves on the bus. We wrote each other lots of letters, crimped our hair, took photos in graveyards, played Cure songs on her Casio keyboard and planned how to make our bedrooms more goth with the help of the Gothic Martha Stewart website.

Both of us had been drawn to goth from feelings of being an outsider, in Natasha's case even more so, as she grew up in a country area where there was little alternative to farming culture. She had left the farm and was now studying in Wollongong but my life was fairly aimless, still hampered by fatigue. In plotting our future, we decided we'd make our living selling sheep skulls, gathered from her parents' farm, at Glebe Markets. This would ensure our goth notoriety as well as our income.

Our clothing and musical tastes were unmistakably goth, we knew how to pronounce Einstürzende Neubauten and we had read Nick Cave's *And the Ass Saw the Angel*, but we still suffered feelings of inferiority when it came to going to clubs. The first time I went goth

clubbing I had made the novice's error of appearing before midnight. I went to Shrine, which was held in a dungeon-like room underneath the Agincourt Hotel by UTS on Broadway. There were only a few people in the club and just one person on the dancefloor, a man in a brown suit moonwalking to 'Black Planet' by The Sisters of Mercy. I cursed myself for waiting until I was 18, if this was what goth clubs had been reduced to.

I needed only to wait a few more hours, until after midnight. Then the dance floor was filled with goths, arms flailing as if struggling to be free of ever falling cobwebs. Others clustered in groups, sipping from bottles of Sub Zero, a vodka premix that came in a long thin bottle. Some asked for a Sub Zero with a dash of grenadine in it, to colour it blood-red.

Goth clubs had a clandestine atmosphere, dark dens thick with the smell of hairspray, dry ice and clove cigarettes. I'd often feel nervous going in and facing the goth girl guarding the entrance, as if I might be denied entry. These girls used the moniker 'door bitch' with pride and their tough aura was cultivated to dissuade subculture tourists wearing blue jeans. Once, at the desk behind which the door bitch presided, a taxidermy rat mounted on a red velvet plinth was on display. My curiosity about the creature overcame my shyness and I asked about it. 'Someone traded it for entry,' she told me. 'They didn't have any money, so they gave me the rat instead.'

I related my goth club stories in letters to Natasha, and sometimes she would travel to Sydney and we'd visit a club, or see a band together. One night we set out for Newtown to see Neuropaque, a Sydney band with lugubrious, Christian Death-inspired songs. We got ready at Matt's apartment, listening to records as we smoked clove cigarettes on the balcony. Often the fun and anticipation of getting ready to go out far outweighed the joy of the actual event. I dressed in the Birthday Party T-shirt I'd recently bought for $5 at Glebe Markets. The shirt had been cut down the sides with eyelets sewn in which were then laced up with black string. The fabric was soft and old, and I wondered at the shirt's life, having come all the way from Bremen in 1982, as was written on the back of the shirt. Although I would have been four when the show the shirt commemorated took place, I felt very authentic wearing it. Natasha wore a long, black gown she had sewn from lacy fabric, and we both wore strings of black rosary beads.

Before we left we took photos on the balcony, leaning against the railing and the red bricks of the apartment complex. Suburban Sydney stretched all around us in a uniform web of streets and buildings, but our small part of the universe felt intense and dynamic.

The gig was at Feedback, a bar and venue above the railway line at Newtown station. Feedback was legendary among goths after Nick Cave made a surprise appearance at a Dirty Three show there in early 1995 to sing 'Running Scared' and 'Tupelo'. A cassette bootleg of the show circulated, further confirming the night's iconic status.

The only appearance of Nick Cave on the Neuropaque night was on the front of my Birthday Party shirt. Natasha and I waited for the doors to open, sitting in a doorway, sipping the sweet, sticky Blackberry Nip we'd planned to smuggle in and watching people pass by on King Street. Rachael, arriving for the Neuropaque show, took a photo of us leaning to either side of the doorway, rolling our eyes, our dark red lips stern.

Once inside Feedback we sat on the floor among the other goths as if we were at a school assembly. Although at goth clubs the dancefloor was usually full of people doing their best bat or

gravedigger impressions, often when bands played people sat coolly reserved, watching. As Neuropaque played a song called 'Skeller Sex Passion' the singer wound the microphone cord around his neck like a noose. Watching this I felt an unexpected moment of communion with the people who surrounded us, the haughty ice-queen girls, the skinny boys wearing fishnet stockings on their arms, the girls with a metre of red and black plaits trailing down their backs, even the guy wearing the Sisters of Mercy 'Fuck Me and Marry Me Young' T-shirt.

Later, as Natasha and I waited at Railway Square for a bus back to the suburbs, we talked about the band she was starting with two goth boys in Wollongong and laughed about its provisional title: TGPM, Three Goths Play Music. They didn't have many songs but they did already have a series of band photographs, in which Natasha posed with a parasol, a key goth object we thought might be another good thing to sell at our Glebe Markets skull stall. I had sourced white parasols in a Chinatown gift shop, all we needed was some packets of black Dylon.

Despite our plans we never became goth entrepreneurs. A year later Natasha died of leukaemia and I then spent months in my room at my first sharehouse, a thick green curtain blocking out the light, listening to The Church and Throwing Muses records on a cheap, three-in-one stereo with a turntable that revolved slightly too fast. At night I'd go and visit my friend Ryan who worked at the service station on the corner, or I'd venture into the 24-hour Kinkos on Liverpool Street in the city to do some photocopying. The Kinkos was always inhabited by at least one conspiracy theorist photocopying tracts about aliens, someone making flyers for their band or dance party, or people like me making zines.

One night I was loitering outside the Kinkos when a man came up to me and stopped. He looked at my outfit of black lace and layers of petticoats and asked, meanly, 'Why are you wearing all black? Has someone died?'

'Yes,' I said. 'My best friend died. These are her clothes.'

As he spluttered apologies, offering me cigarettes and saying he didn't mean to be rude, my thoughts drifted away from him, away from

Kinkos and out into the ether, searching for the subtlest of feelings that something of Natasha hovered around me. But there was just an emptiness.

For all my earlier wonderings about how I would live my adult life, here I was, living in a Camperdown share house with Matt and Vic and sleeping the days away. The house had the cast iron plate and strings from a grand piano leaning up in the hallway beside the front door, and the zithery sound of people plucking the strings would reach up to me as I lay in bed. Vic would listen to the Laughing Clowns album *Ghosts of an Ideal Wife* on repeat and say the line 'the saddest girl I know' was about me.

When I did come downstairs to the living room a record would be playing in the corner, Die Haut or The Birthday Party, the ashtrays full and some kind of plan would be developing. Sometimes this involved driving to Darlinghurst to buy vegie burgers, other times it meant going to see bands, often in pubs but also in more unusual places. One night we went to see Alien Christ, a band given to dark, intense explosions of noise at unexpected points in their songs. The show was in what was usually a bondage dungeon, with rings and hooks set into the black walls. I was sitting at the side of the room on top of some kind of device that looked like a pommel horse, when a man came up to me and declared, 'You're a cat'. He would not be dissuaded on the point that

I had a feline soul – I was thankful when the band escalated into one of their explosions of sound that made more talking impossible.

Sometimes we'd make a household excursion to a goth club. Whenever this happened Matt and Vic would insist on calling each other their goth names, Noir and Pablo, and speaking in high, strained voices as if unable to cope with the pain inside. Although they often made fun of it, they both had an affection for goth culture, and were well known in the scene. I'd sometimes help Vic devise new, more preposterous dances, the more ridiculous the better. The gravedigger was all well and good, but what about crawling around on the dance floor and trying to bite people's ankles? Other times I'd sit morosely drinking vodka until a song by the Virgin Prunes came on, which I'd have to dance to, no matter what.

The Virgin Prunes album *If I Die, I Die* was my favourite goth album, and one particularly peppy song from it, 'Baby Turns Blue', was often played at clubs. The Virgin Prunes were an Irish band with two singers, Guggi and Gavin Friday. Matt owned a live video of the Virgin Prunes called *Sons Find Devils*, although after watching it once he declared he never would again, it did his head in. This was what I liked about it. In their performances both men prowled the stage, exchanging lines of the song as if they were two parts of one restless mind. When they were teenagers the members of the band were part of a small gang of Dublin misfits who called themselves Lypton Village, of which the most well known member was Bono, who went on to form U2. The Virgin Prunes were nothing like U2. They wore dresses and their songs sounded as if they had been recorded in the corridors of an asylum, some of them gentle, others howling and fierce. On the back cover of the album was a photograph of them mud smeared, almost naked, stepping across a still, black stream. I didn't understand it but I appreciated its genuine weirdness.

If I Die, I Die has become my goth time capsule. When I listen to it I am back among the dry ice and clove-cigarette smoke, or sitting in my room listening to *Sacrament* on the radio, or digging through a serpent's nest of black clothes looking for a spiderweb lace shirt, as if no time at all has passed between then and now.

It wasn't long after I moved away from the Camperdown house that the goth influences in my life began to recede, although I still went to goth parties sometimes. At one there were cardboard gravestones among the long grass in the garden. At another a goth boy insisted on showing me his diary, and sat by me as I read pages of his misery-fuelled musings before asking 'What do you think?' I asked if he could wait a minute and fled into the living room, where a group of guys were dancing to 'We Are the Pigs' by Suede.

Soon I was in a new phase, dancing to Francoise Hardy songs at indie pop clubs and wearing 70s dresses in explosive colours. I bought a lot of albums on Flying Nun records, atmospheric pop from Dunedin like The Chills and The Verlaines, music that made me think of frosty mornings and thick jumpers. While I was no happier ør sadder than I had been in my goth years, the colourful clothes and three-minute pop songs did make me feel brighter, more awake.

I had been buying op-shop dresses that broke with my strict goth palette of black, electric blue, red, pink and white. My favourite outfit was a pale blue polyester dress with multicoloured spots all over it, long strings of plastic beads, white knee socks and Mary Janes. I felt like an oversized cartoon schoolgirl in this outfit as I listened to Pulp and Belle and Sebastian, or the sugar-rush songs of twee pop bands like Talulah Gosh and Heavenly.

One day I considered the inches of black bangles on my wrists. I had worn them for so long continuously that they had shrunk and were no longer able to fit over my hands. I found a pair of long scissors and cut the bangles off, revealing my pale wrists to the light.

Yet the goth part of me has never completely disappeared. My hair is still long and black. I keep well stocked with black eyeliner. Every so often I put on the Virgin Prunes and dance around like I'm fighting back cobwebs.

End of the Century

I set out from my house in Annandale and began to trace a haphazard path through the back streets. It was a good night to walk. Pipes arranged on walls looked like dancing figures, flowers had delicate names, houses were haunted. It was a Sunday night in 2002. The world hadn't ended, the Y2K bug hadn't destroyed life as I knew it, the Olympics had swept through the city. 2000 had been such a landmark date that I had given little thought to how life might be on the other side. Yet here I was exploring the night streets of Annandale, then Stanmore, then Petersham. I'd lived there for long enough that all these places felt like my own.

I emerged from the back streets onto Parramatta Road. When I walked along Parramatta Road I felt as if I was surveying my domain, checking that all was in order. It was as run down as ever, though it went through constant changes. The dinosaur mural had been painted over and the video store replaced by a Fantastic Furniture. The Loyal Orange op-shop, where I'd once bought 'Bible Greats' action figurines of David and Goliath, had its shutters down permanently.

I walked up as far as Alan Hot Bread, the bakery near the corner of Catherine Street. Stacked up in plastic pallets on the pavement outside, freshly baked loaves of bread cooled. The bakers left the loaves out like this on most nights and I found it strange that they exposed bread to Parramatta Road air. I called them 'road loaves', and imagined eating them to be a kind of Parramatta Road sacrament.

On the way home with my road loaf I turned off Parramatta Road again to walk home through the back streets of Petersham. Rubbish bins were lined up along the streets and alleyways and I came across a suitcase in a pile of junk put out for collection. It was on top of other less interesting rubbish, a broken cash register, a rusty wok, chipped white plates. I unlatched the clasps to see what was inside. There were letters and notes and cards, the kind of personal ephemera that accumulates more with every year, is rarely looked at, but difficult to discard. I closed the locks, swept the suitcase up by the handle and took it home with me.

Later I examined the contents of the case. The papers inside dated from 1990 and belonged to a girl who was in her early twenties at that time. As well as letters there were old leases, x-rays, a diary in a black and red notebook, and pictures with blu-tack stains on the corners that at one time must have been stuck on her walls. This collection was uncannily similar to my own personal papers. Looking through them gave me an eerie feeling. She had lived in share houses in the inner west, her friends played in bands, she kept Christmas cards from her grandparents alongside flyers for anarchist punk gigs.

In one special envelope were love letters from her boyfriend. Their whole relationship was packaged into an A4 envelope from its early, jubilant stages to its final disintegrating moments. She had kept every scrap of paper, the wrapping paper from his gifts, his quickly scribbled notes. He had written her long, stream-of-consciousness stories on foolscap journal paper, cards with hand-drawn cartoons, and long, yearning letters written in neat capital letters. Again and again he professed his love for her, writing poems about how her hands looked in red woollen gloves. At the bottom of the envelope were two brittle braids of his long blonde hair.

I sat on the black and white checkerboard rug in my room, suitcase open in front of me, the blonde braids in my hand feeling as if I had stolen someone else's memories. I was around the same age that she had been in 1990. This gave me an uncomfortable feeling. It was ghostly to imagine my present day life as a past time, although inevitably it would become so.

Why, I wondered, had she decided to get rid of her letters? Maybe she wanted to be free of her past. I understood the feeling. I'd destroyed the teenage diary I'd kept in the index book, it was a reminder of feelings of loneliness I didn't want to remember. Yet it was impossible to be free of my past identities by getting rid of the evidence. I imagined all the previous versions of myself like the layers of a baboushka doll, sitting neatly inside the other, contained within the outermost layer of my current self.

Despite getting rid of my diary I had kept most of my teenage ephemera. Some was stored in suitcases or tins, other things were displayed around the house. My walls were covered in pictures, photographs, notes and posters, so many that first time visitors often exclaimed at the visual chaos of my home environment. Some of the pictures I'd had for a long time: a yellowing photocopy of a Sylvia Plath poem our English teacher had given us to read in high school, 'The Arrival of the Bee Box', was blu-tacked above my desk along with postcards of The Smiths and the 'How Odd' pet tag I used to wear as a necklace. There were hundreds more such pictures and objects covering the walls, both precious and disposable things jumbled up into one big patchwork. I lived in an ever-expanding, personal museum.

The suitcase of another girl's memories would never belong to me. I was merely its custodian and, in the months after finding it, I thought deeply about what I to do with it. I imagined all number of potential scenarios. A heartwarming *Amelie*-style reunion of suitcase and its owner. Her alarm at seeing the suitcase again after having rid herself of it, she thought, forever, and her horror that I had gone through its contents, read her diary and her love letters.

I imagined a stranger looking through my mementos. Once set free from their personal significance, my suitcases of cassettes and papers, letters and photographs, seemed as much trash as they were treasure. I thought of them in a pile of rubbish on the street, rifled through by late-night scavengers. Or rescued by someone with a penchant for lost objects, who saw some reflection of their own life in mine. Or, in hundreds of years' time, discovered by archaeologists, a capsule of life from a time long past.

Index

Acknowledgements

Thank you to Ivor Indyk and Alice Grundy at Giramondo for their support and guidance with this project. Thank you to those who helped with the writing of this book, Simon Yates, Rachael Holt, Beth Taylor and Matt Gear, and to Stephanie Varga who helped me in the writing of the book and also took the photo of me in my hallway in Annandale. Thank you also to everyone whose names appear in the pages of this book for keeping me company through the 1990s.

The idea for *Ninety 9* began with my zine *Band T-Shirt*. Thank you to Luke Sinclair, with whom I had the long conversation about band T-shirts which inspired the zine. Thank you to Sticky Institute, *PAN Magazine* and *Contrappasso Magazine* for inviting me to read band T-shirt stories and in one case throw a band t-shirt tea party, and thank you also to everyone who wrote to me with their own band T-shirt stories.

Thank you for reading *Ninety 9*. If you'd like to write to me, my address is:

Vanessa Berry
PO Box 1879
Strawberry Hills NSW 2012
Australia

Biographical Note

After living through the 1990s Vanessa Berry has continued to make zines, including *I am a Camera* and *Disposable Camera*. In 2007 a selection of her zine writing was collected in the book *Strawberry Hills Forever*, and her zines have been exhibited in galleries in Australia and internationally. She is the author of two blogs about Sydney, *Biblioburbia* and *Mirror Sydney*.